LÉVI-STRAUSS

PROFESSOR SIR EDMUND LEACH (1910–1989) was
educated at Marlborough College and Clare College,
Cambridge, and served in Burma during the Second
World War. He taught anthropology first at the London
School of Economics, and then at Cambridge. Edmund
Leach was Professor of Social Anthropology in the
University of Cambridge from 1972 to 1978, and Provost
of King's College Cambridge from 1966 to 1979. He was
twice Vice-President, and then President (from 1971 to
1975) of the Royal Anthropological Institute. His
anthropological fieldwork was chiefly in Burma, Taiwan,
Kurdistan and Sri Lanka. In addition to his professional
anthropological writings, he wrote, reviewed, lectured
and broadcast very widely, and was probably the
best-known British anthropologist of his generation. His
published works include *Political Systems of Highland
Burma* (1954), *Pul Eliya: A Village in Ceylon* (1969),
Rethinking Anthropology (1961), *Genesis as Myth* (1969),
A Runaway World? (1968; the text of his controversial
1967 Reith Lectures), *Culture and Communication* (1976),
Social Anthropology (1982) and, with D. Alan Aycock,
Structuralist Analysis of Biblical Myth (1983).

JAMES LAIDLAW is a Senior Research Fellow of King's
College, Cambridge, and an Assistant Lecturer in the
Department of Social Anthropology, University of
Cambridge. His publications include *Riches and
Renunciation: Religion, Economy and Society among
the Jains* (1995) and, with Caroline Humphrey, *The
Archetypal Actions of Ritual: A Theory of Ritual
Illustrated by the Jain Rite of Worship* (1994).

Modern Masters

Lévi-Strauss

FOURTH EDITION

Edmund Leach

With a new Introduction and
revised Notes and Guide to Further Reading
by James Laidlaw

 FontanaPress
An Imprint of HarperCollins*Publishers*

Fontana Press
An imprint of HarperCollins*Publishers*
77–85 Fulham Palace Road,
Hammersmith, London W6 8JB

Fourth edition 1996
1   3   5   7   9   8   6   4   2

First published in Great Britain by
Fontana Paperbacks 1970
Second Edition 1974
Third Edition 1985

ISBN 0 00 686330-2

Set in Postscript Linotype Trump Medieval by
Rowland Phototypesetting Ltd
Bury St Edmunds, Suffolk

Printed and bound in Great Britain by
Caledonian International Book Manufacturing Ltd, Glasgow

Contents

Acknowledgments

For permission to quote from works in copyright acknowledgment is due to the following: to Basic Books Inc., Publishers, New York, for extracts from *Structural Anthropology* by Claude Lévi-Strauss, translated by Claire Jacobson and Brooke Grundfest Schoepf; to the author and Messrs Hutchinson and Co. (Publishers) Ltd, London, for extracts from *World on the Wane* by Claude Lévi-Strauss; to the author, Messrs Jonathan Cape Ltd, London, and Harper & Row, Publishers, Inc., New York, for extracts from the first three volumes of *Mythologiques* by Claude Lévi-Strauss, translated from the French by permission of Harper & Row; to Jonathan Cape Ltd, London, for a diagram from *Elements of Semiology* by Roland Barthes, translated by Annette Lavers and Colin Smith; to the Merlin Press Ltd, London, and Beacon Press, Boston, for extracts from *Totemism* by Claude Lévi-Strauss; to the Royal Anthropological Institute of Great Britain and Ireland, London for an extract from 'The Future of Kinship Studies', the Huxley Memorial Lecture by Claude Lévi-Strauss, in *Proceedings of the Royal Anthropological Institute*, 1965; to Tavistock Publications, London, for an extract from *The Structural Study of Myth and Totemism*, edited by E. R. Leach; to Weidenfeld (Publishers) Ltd, London, for extracts from *The Savage Mind* by Claude Lévi-Strauss; to Abelard-Schuman Ltd, for extracts from *Tristes Tropiques* by Claude Lévi-Strauss (New York: Criterion Books), 1961.

Introduction
by James Laidlaw

'Claude Lévi-Strauss, Professor of Social Anthropology at the Collège de France, is, by common consent, the most distinguished exponent of this particular academic trade to be found anywhere outside the English speaking world, but . . .'

With these words Edmund Leach begins his little book on the founder and prophet of Structuralism, and they set a tone that persists throughout. Although this tone is rather puzzling at first, attending to it helps us to see how best to read the book, and how to get most out of it.

It is striking that even as he is advertising the importance of his subject matter, Leach mixes his superlatives and honorifics with equivocation and qualification, and by a slight parody of high seriousness he adds a touch of mockery. Although Lévi-Strauss is to be regarded, by editorial decree, as being the 'Modern Master', Leach refuses to engage with him on any terms other than those of an equal. His purpose is not – or only very secondarily – one of exegesis. It isn't even critical exegesis. The focus of this book is not on the subtleties of what Lévi-Strauss, the individual, thinks about this or that matter, but on determining what ideas are essential to Structuralism, in showing just what the Structuralist method of analysis consists of and why it is distinctive, and in trying to establish whether the gain in understanding is worth all the trouble and justifies all the fuss.

So Leach's imagined reader is not the potential disciple of an up-to-the-minute intellectual guru (and since we are now twenty-five years on, that is just as well) but a serious and critical student, and perhaps even more a colleague from another discipline – a classicist, say, leaning across the lunch table at King's College in Cambridge and demanding to know in plain English what 'this Structuralism business' is all about. Is it really a serious method of analysis which everyone ought to be informed about, and if so, how does it work? And if it were applied, say, to Greek mythology, would it tell us something we don't already know? Leach clearly thought that much of Lévi-Strauss' writing was open to serious objection – empirical, theoretical, and on grounds of rank obscurity. But he thought the answer to the second of these questions was 'yes'; and this book sets out to justify that opinion, by trying to answer the first.

Edmund Leach the anthropologist was closely associated, almost from the first, with the name of Lévi-Strauss. This happened partly by coincidence. Leach had begun anthropological fieldwork in the Burma hills in 1939 (fieldwork which, in the event, had to be combined with behind-the-lines military service in the area). He returned at the end of the war and wrote up his doctoral dissertation, but as he began publishing the results of this research there appeared, in 1949, Lévi-Strauss' first great anthropological treatise, *Les Structures élémentaires de la parenté*, which proposed nothing less than a general theory of the foundations of human culture and society, together with a sweeping classification of forms of social structure. And it so happened that the Kachin, the people who had been the subject of Leach's fieldwork, occupied a pivotal place in the argument of that book. They were one of two peoples – the other being the Gilyak of eastern Siberia – whose marriage system represented for Lévi-Strauss clear and paradigmatic cases of what he called 'generalized exchange'. This notion of generalized exchange (which Leach explains in Chapter 6 of this book) was arguably the volume's most important theoretical idea. And the Kachin, being already much better documented than the Gilyak, are the principal medium through which it is expounded.

Leach was already rethinking his first attempts to understand Kachin social structure, and he seems to have been captivated almost immediately by the force and elegance of Lévi-Strauss' analysis. But at the same time he was infuriated by what he saw as unforgivable blunders with the ethnographic facts. Lévi-Strauss' ambitions were too grand and all-embracing, and his concern with the Kachin data was driven too forcibly by the requirements of his larger argument. He seemed to think, for instance, that a husband's kin group ranked higher than that of his wife, when in fact the reverse is the case. But worse than this, he didn't seem to Leach to care much *which* of these was true, because it didn't make any difference to his model. And yet, the fact that he was so cavalier with the data only made his theoretical achievement – the fact that he had seen how the system really worked – all the more impressive.

The first of Leach's anthropological publications to achieve really widespread notice (Leach 1951) was, substantially, a critical analysis on his Kachin data of the lessons he had drawn from Lévi-Strauss, albeit with some strongly-worded statements of what he took to be the latter's faults. And his major book on the Kachin (1954) was even more profoundly in sympathy with Lévi-Strauss' style of analysis: his concept of social structure and his use of a mathematical notion of a model. Later, in the 1960s, as Lévi-Strauss' writings on totemism and mythology started to appear,

9

Leach too turned his attention to systems of social classification and to the structural analysis of myth.

I do not mean to imply that Leach simply borrowed Lévi-Strauss' ideas. Leach's position was always distinctive, and his own contributions to the study of social structure, symbolism and myth (especially the analysis of biblical myth), as well as his observations on contemporary society and culture, were provocative and original. (Indeed, a 'Modern Master' on Leach himself would not have been out of place.) His ideas seem to have developed in an always engaged and, on Leach's side at any rate, an always heated dialogue with those of Lévi-Strauss. However, as the vogue for Structuralism grew, Leach did increasingly come to be seen as an expositor of Lévi-Strauss. He reviewed most of the latter's major works as they appeared, in the literary and political weeklies. And by the late 1960s the anxiety of influence is certainly discernible. In 1967, the year in which Leach himself achieved public notoriety with his controversial Reith Lectures, he wrote a piece for the *New York Review of Books.* He may have been preparing this volume at the time – some short passages in the two are practically identical – and in this review the concern to demonstrate his independence is explicit: 'I have put in that cautionary paragraph', he wrote, 'for the benefit of my anthropological colleagues, some of whom seem to think that I am such a devoted Lévi-Straussian that I can no longer exercise any scholarly detachment on the subject at all' (Leach 1967). In this volume Leach shows, clearly enough, that he is not just a 'devoted Lévi-Straussian', but the way he does so is the very opposite of 'scholarly detachment'. On the contrary, the great strengths of the book depend on its intensely personal presentation of the ideas.

The distinctive thing about this book – and it explains

the tone I mentioned at the outset – is the extent which the Lévi-Strauss presented here is *Leach's* Lévi-Strauss: the one he was inspired and enraged by. Of course, something of the sort must always be the case. Any author of a book of this kind has to select, and the selection is bound to be personal. But I mean rather more than this. When Leach sets out to explain one of Lévi-Strauss' ideas, he does so by explaining what use and enlightenment he, Edmund Leach, has got from it. This isn't always explicit. For instance in Chapter 3, when he is explaining Lévi-Strauss' approach to totemic classifications, Leach illustrates the key idea of a structural homology between two systems of differences, with an example which although he doesn't mention it, comes from one of his own essays, on animal classification in England (1964). To be sure, that essay was inspired by Lévi-Strauss' writings, but it is the ideas *as Leach has assimilated and used them* that the reader is led through.

At one point in the book Leach describes himself as 'imitating' Lévi-Strauss. But really he's doing rather more than that, because he is personally quite committed to the kind of Structuralist analysis he illustrates. This positive demonstration of a method is juxtaposed with repeated expressions of disagreement with Lévi-Strauss. And it's the method, most importantly, that the disagreements are about. Leach keeps his dialogue with Lévi-Strauss in the foreground of the book, and this is in order to draw the reader actively into the argument. Now, he says repeatedly, you're going to have to think that point through, and decide for yourself what to make of it.

In these ways Leach achieves, I think, what must be the most difficult objective of an introductory study. He enables the reader to glimpse how it might be possible to do the same, to use the ideas and the method in one's own work.

And for anyone wishing seriously to come to grips with Lévi-Strauss' thought, this is of the greatest possible value.

There are costs attached to this strategy, and readers should of course be no more uncritically trusting of Leach, than he advises them to be with Lévi-Strauss. Certainly there are aspects of Leach's presentation that are decidedly idiosyncratic. He begins by locating Lévi-Strauss in relation to Frazer and Malinowski. Both these authors are (or were) well-known and widely-read in the English-speaking world, so this will indeed be helpful to many readers; but while both figures were persistently important intellectual reference-points for Leach himself, neither has ever been of more than incidental interest to Lévi-Strauss. And sometimes Leach is unfair. He carps about how little fieldwork Lévi-Strauss has done, and drives the point home with the observation that the latter's sponsor for his early professorship in Brazil, Celestin Bouglé, had written a book about caste without having visited India. In this way he rather gives the impression of a whole intellectual world of armchair social scientists in which Lévi-Strauss was comfortably ensconced. But in fact the point is borrowed from Lévi-Strauss himself, who had written it, as a criticism of Bouglé, decades before (T.T.E.: 56). Perhaps most puzzling is the almost intemperately critical tone of the chapter on kinship. This is odd, since Leach had earlier derived such stimulation from this work, and had even regretted Lévi-Strauss' desertion of the field of kinship – 'the hard core' of anthropology, as he put it – to take up the study of myth in 'the land of the Lotus Eaters' (Leach 1967). It seems that his attitude hardened after the publication of the revised edition of *Les Structures élémentaires* (1967), when all the empirical objections raised by Leach and others were dismissed by Lévi-Strauss as not affecting the argument. Or perhaps Leach had just ceased to be engaged by ideas he had so fully assimilated, and his attention was still held only by the flaws.

When this book was first written Structuralism was the height of intellectual fashion. This indeed is why it was one of the first five in the Modern Masters series – along with Albert Camus, Franz Fanon, Herbert Marcuse and (it *was* a long time ago!) Che Guevara. So Leach obviously felt he had to call for caution, just as much as he had to communicate his own intellectual excitement. He focused on the basic ideas, and most especially on the method, for these he thought had lasting value. This is why this book retains its usefulness long after the vogue for Structuralism has past.

It's an obvious point, and one that follows directly from what I've been saying, that for all the same reasons that this is an entertaining and thought-provoking introduction to Lévi-Strauss and a good thing to read *in tandem* with some of his own work, for just those reasons it is disastrous and almost uniquely transparent, when it is used as a crib. But perhaps it is also tempting to use it this way, because it's so full of highly repeatable arguments and also, perhaps, because Leach does exaggerate somewhat the difficulty of reading Lévi-Strauss. When this happens, it is a pity, not only because students then write bad essays, but because they miss the pleasure of reading Lévi-Strauss, a pleasure for which, in his singular way, Leach in this book prepares them rather well.

Editor's Note

This book was first published in 1970, slightly revised in 1974, and then republished, with a new Note on Further Reading, in 1985. In the years since Leach wrote this book, Lévi-Strauss has published a great deal of new work (see References), but his intellectual project has been one of remarkable consistency. These recent works add greatly to Lévi-Strauss' achievements (indeed, my principal recommendation for further reading is among them), but the fundamentals of his method and approach have not changed. For this reason, and also because this book is, in its own right, an important document in the history of anthropological thought, I have left Leach's revised text virtually untouched, except for the correction of some obvious errors.

I have added references to the English translations of Lévi-Strauss' writings, where Leach chose to cite only the French, or where a translation has become available only since he wrote. I have not altered Leach's own translations, or replaced them with subsequently published versions. I have added some notes of my own, either to bring the story up to date, to add some background information, or to alert the reader to a particularly debatable judgement. These notes are enclosed in square brackets and begin with my initials (JAL). I have brought up to date the Chronology in Chapter 1, and the References, and written a new Note on Further Reading.
J A L (August, 1995)

1   The Man Himself

Claude Lévi-Strauss, Professor of Social Anthropology at the Collège de France, is, by common consent, the most distinguished exponent of this particular academic trade to be found anywhere outside the English speaking world, but scholars who call themselves social anthropologists are of two kinds. The prototype of the first was the late Sir James Frazer (1854–1941), author of *The Golden Bough*. He was a man of monumental learning who had no first hand acquaintance with the lives of the primitive peoples about whom he wrote. He hoped to discover fundamental truths about the nature of human psychology by comparing the details of human culture on a world wide scale. The prototype of the second was Bronislaw Malinowski (1884–1942), born in Poland but naturalized an Englishman, who spent most of his academic life analysing the results of research which he himself had personally conducted over a period of four years, in a single small village in far off Melanesia. His aim was to show how this exotic community 'functioned' as a social system and how its individual members passed through their lives from the cradle to the grave. He was more interested in the differences between human cultures than in their overall similarity.

Most of those who at present call themselves social anthropologists either in Britain or the United States claim to be 'functionalists'; broadly speaking they are anthropologists in the style and tradition of Malinowski. In contrast,

Lévi-Strauss

Claude Lévi-Strauss is a social anthropologist in the tradition though not in the style of Frazer. His ultimate concern is to establish facts which are true about 'the human mind', rather than about the organization of any particular society or class of societies. The difference is fundamental.

In his day Malinowski had three kinds of celebrity. His renown among the general public was as a prophet of free love. Though tame by modern standards, his accounts of the sexual eccentricities of Trobriand Islanders were rated as near pornography. The almost passionate enthusiasm of professional colleagues rested on other grounds, firstly the novelty of his methods of field research which have now been universally imitated, secondly the dogmas of his special brand of 'functionalism', an oversimplified mechanistic style of sociological theorizing now generally viewed with some contempt.

Lévi-Strauss' record has been quite different. From the very start he has been a straight scholar-intellectual. Apart from some engaging photographs of naked Amazonian ladies tucked in at the end of *Tristes Tropiques* (1955), he has refrained from popularizing gimmicks of the kind which led Malinowski to entitle one of his Trobriand monographs *The Sexual Life of Savages*. By Malinowski standards Lévi-Strauss' field research is of only moderate quality. The outstanding characteristic of his writing, whether in French or in English, is that it is difficult to understand; his sociological theories combine baffling complexity with overwhelming erudition. Some readers even suspect that they are being treated to a confidence trick. Even now, despite his immense prestige, the critics among his professional colleagues still greatly outnumber the disciples. Yet his academic importance is unquestioned. Lévi-Strauss is admired not so much for the novelty of his ideas as for the bold originality with which he seeks to apply them. He has suggested new ways of looking at familiar facts; it is the method that is interesting rather than the practical consequences of the use to which it has been put.

The method, as such, is as much linguistic as anthropological and it has aroused excitement among many different brands of intellectual, students of literature, of politics, of ancient philosophy, of theology, of art. The purpose of this book is to give some indication of why this should be so. But first I must declare a personal prejudice.

I myself was once a pupil of Malinowski and I am, at heart, still a 'functionalist' even though I recognize the limitations of Malinowski's own brand of theory. Although I have occasionally used the 'structuralist' methods of Lévi-Strauss to illuminate particular features of particular cultural systems the gap between my general position and that of Lévi-Strauss is very wide. This difference of viewpoint is bound to show through in the pages which follow. My main task is to give an account of Lévi-Strauss' methods and opinions rather than to offer private comments, but I cannot pretend to be a disinterested observer.

My concern is with Lévi-Strauss' ideas, not his life history, but since his bibliography, starting in 1936, already includes eleven books and well over 100 substantial articles I have a formidable task.[1] No-one could survey such a landscape without introducing distortions and I am going to make matters even worse by ignoring the chronology. I shall start in the middle and work both forwards and backwards. There is a personal justification for this eccentricity which needs to be explained.

We may think of Lévi-Strauss's writings as a three-pointed star radiating around the autobiographical ethnographic travel book *Tristes Tropiques* (1955). The three limbs of the star would then be labelled: (i) kinship theory, (ii) the logic of myth, (iii) the theory of primitive classification. In my biased estimation the first of these, which is also the earliest, is the least important. This is a value judgement which our author himself does not share. In his later writings Lévi-Strauss frequently refers back to *Les Structures élémentaires de la parenté* (1949) as if it were an authoritative landmark in the history of social anthropology and the substantially revised English language edition (1969) includes a vigorous polemical counter-attack against the views of those English admirers like myself who have dared to suggest that parts of his theory do not fit the facts.

Obviously a book of this sort cannot provide me with a base from which to develop a sympathetic commentary on Lévi-Strauss' general attitude. So I shall leave it until the end. Meanwhile we need a chronological guideline. Table A provides dates for a series of significant events.

TABLE A *Chronology of the Life of Lévi-Strauss*[a]

Year

1908	Born in Belgium
1914–18	Lived with his parents (his father was an artist) near Versailles
1927–32	Student in University of Paris, where he took a degree in Law with *agrégation* in Philosophy. His reading included works 'by the masters of the French School of Sociology' – presumably Saint-Simon, Comte, Durkheim, Mauss[b]
1934	Through the patronage of Celestin Bouglé,[c] Director of the École Normale Superieure, was offered a post as Professor of Sociology at the University of São Paulo, Brazil

1934–37 Professor of Sociology, University of São Paulo[d]. During this period he seems to have returned to France on several occasions. He also made several brief visits to the interior of Brazil to engage in ethnographic investigations. By the end of the period he had had about five months of actual field experience

1934 Read Lowie: *Primitive Society* (1920) in English; this was his first introduction to specialist anthropological writing. E. Metraux's French translation of Lowie's book was not published until 1935

1936 First anthropological publication: a 45-page article on the social organization of the Bororo Indians

1938–39 Having resigned from the service of the University of São Paulo he obtained French Government financial support for a more extensive expedition to central Brazil. The details of the expedition are hard to determine. Lévi-Strauss initially had two scientific companions engaged in other kinds of research. The party left its base at Cuiaba in June 1938 and reached the junction of the Madeira and Machado rivers by the end of the year. They seem to have been on the move nearly the whole time. Everything that Lévi-Strauss has written about the Nambikwara and Tupi-Kawahib Indians seems to be based on this experience

1939–40 In France on military service

1941 (Spring) Made his way via Martinique and Puerto Rico to New York to take up a post at the New School for Social Research engineered for him by Robert Lowie, E. Metraux and Max Ascoli

1945 Contributed article 'L'analyse structurale en linguistique et en anthropologie' to *Word: Journal of the Linguistic Circle of New York* (founded by Roman Jakobson and his associates)

1946–47 French Cultural Attaché in the United States

1948 *La Vie familiale et sociale des Indiens Nambikwara* (Paris: Société des Américanistes)

1949	*Les Structures élémentaires de la parenté* (First Edition, Paris: P.U.F.)
1950	Director of Studies at the École pratique des hautes études, University of Paris (Laboratory of Social Anthropology) (E.P.H.E.)
1950	Short fieldwork trip to Chittagong, East Pakistan
1952	*Race and History* (Paris: UNESCO)
1953–60	Secretary General of the International Council of Social Sciences
1955	'The Structural Study of Myth', *Journal of American Folklore*, Vol. 68, No. 270, pp. 428–44, and *Tristes Tropiques* (Paris: Plon)
1958	*Anthropologie Structurale* (Paris: Plon)
1959	Appointed to Chair of Social Anthropology at the Collège de France
1960	'La Geste d'Asdiwal' (*Annuaire de l' E.P.H.E.*, 5me section, Sciences Religieuses, 1958–59; Paris)
1962	*Le Totémisme aujourd'hui* and *La Pensée sauvage*
1964	*Mythologiques*, Vol. I: *Le Cru et le cuit*. Officer of the Legion of Honour
1967	*Mythologiques*, Vol. II: *Du Miel aux cendres*
1967	*Mythologiques*, Vol. III: *L'Origine des manières de table*
1968	Awarded the Gold Medal of the Centre National de la Recherche Scientifique 'the highest French scientific distinction'
1971	*Mythologiques*, Vol. IV: *L'Homme nu* Commander, National Order of Merit
	Anthropologie structuale deux
1973	Member of the French Academy
1975	*La Voie des masques*
1982	Retires from Chair of Social Anthropology at the Collège de France
1983	*Le Regarde éloigné*

1984   *Paroles données*

1985   La Potière jalouse

1991   *Histoire de Lynx*

1993   *Regarder, écouter, lire*

a. Sources are various; down to 1941 most of the information comes from *Tristes Tropiques*. The author is indebted to Professor Lévi-Strauss for some corrections to the text as first issued.

b. Lévi-Strauss also recalls that from a very early age he had been intensely interested in geology and that in late adolescence he developed an interest, first in psycho-analysis, and then in Marxism.

c. Boulgé had earlier been associated with Emile Durkheim and the *l'Année sociologique*. By academic profession he was a philosopher but his reputation rests on a treatise on the Indian Caste System the first version of which appeared in 1900. Bouglé himself never visited India.

d. The University had been founded by French initiative and the French diplomatic mission was still concerned with the recruitment of staff. Lévi-Strauss claims that he caused some consternation among his French colleagues because of his heretical attitude to the functionalist teachings of Durkheim and his interest in the works of the American ethnologists Boas, Kroeber and Lowie.

One further biographical fact which seeps through into a number of Lévi-Strauss writings, notably in the Introduction (*'ouverture'*) and intricately arranged chapter headings of *Mythologiques* I is that he is a gifted musician.

Footnote [b] to Table A deserves further elaboration. In *Tristes Tropiques* (1955) Lévi-Strauss describes Geology, Psycho-analysis and Marxism as his 'three mistresses', making it quite clear that Geology was his first love.

I will come back to the Geology in a moment but first let us glance at his Marxism. Lévi-Strauss himself remarks that:

'Marxism seemed to me to proceed in the same way as geology and psycho-analysis ... All three showed that understanding consists in the reduction of one type of reality to another; that true reality is never the most obvious of realities ... in all these cases the problem is the same: the relation ... between reason and sense-perception ...' (W.W.: 61; T.T.E.: 70).

In practice, the relevance of Marxist ideology for an understanding of Lévi-Strauss is difficult to determine. Lévi-Strauss' use of dialectic, with the formal sequence of thesis–antithesis–synthesis, is Hegelian rather than Marxist and his attitude to history seems to be quite contrary to Marxist dogma. But the picture is greatly confused by the dialectical interplay between the Existentialism of Sartre and the Structuralism of Lévi-Strauss.

Lévi-Strauss first met Sartre in the flesh in New York in 1946 but they had earlier mutual acquaintances. Thus Simone de Beauvoir and Maurice Merleau-Ponty were both fellow student teachers with Lévi-Strauss at the Lycée Janson de Sailly, (P.C.). Articles by Lévi-Strauss have often appeared in Sartre's journal *Les Temps Modernes*, but it would seem that by 1955 personal relations between the two men were distinctly strained. In *Tristes Tropiques* Lévi-Strauss remarks of Existentialism that:

'To promote private preoccupations to the rank of philosophical problems is dangerous and may end in a kind of shop-girl's philosophy' (W.W.: 62 T.T.E.:71).

and the whole of Chapter 9 of *La Pensée sauvage* is devoted to a polemical attack against Sartre's *Critique de la raison dialectique*. Lévi-Strauss is especially scornful of Sartre's (apparent) opinion that the members of exotic societies must necessarily be incapable of intellectual analysis and powers of rational demonstration. Nevertheless he has to admit that:

'he feels himself very close to Sartre whenever the latter applies himself with incomparable artistry, to grasping, in its dialectical movement, a present or past social experience within our own culture' (S.M.: 250).

But then Sartre is a Marxist; and so also, from time to time, is Lévi-Strauss – or so he says! Both authors freely bespatter their pages with Marxist terminology and denounce the other's misuse of the sacred jargon. On this matter I can do no more than draw the reader's attention to a commentary by Jean Pouillon (1965) which is strongly reminiscent of Lewis Carroll's account of the non-battle between Tweedledum and Tweedledee.

I am not trying to suggest that Lévi-Strauss' present position is at all close to that of the Existentialists; on the contrary it is, in many respects, very remote. But Existentialism and Lévi-Strauss' brand of Structuralism have common Marxist roots and the distinction between the two is by no means as sharp as some would like to believe[2]. Despite the savage attack on Sartre, *La Pensée sauvage* is dedicated to the memory of Maurice Merleau-Ponty, the Phenomenologist philosopher, whose position was, on the face of it, very much closer to Existentialism than to Structuralism.

The squabble with Sartre over 'history' is very similar to the squabble with Ricoeur over 'hermeneutic' (Ricoeur: 1963). It stems from a different evaluation of the 'arrow of time'. For the Phenomenologists and the Existentialists, history provides the myth which justifies the present, but the present is also a necessary culmination of where history has brought us to. The Structuralist position is much less egocentric: history offers us images of past societies which were structural transformations of those we know, neither better nor worse. We, in our vantage point of the present, are not in a privileged position of superiority. But Lévi-Strauss' own attitude to history is elusive and I can only advise the persistent enquirer to consult for himself the densely argued pp. 256–64 of *The Savage Mind* (1966).

Two features in Lévi-Strauss' position seem crucial. Firstly he holds that the study of history diachronically and the study of anthropology cross-culturally but synchronically are two alternative ways of doing the same kind of thing:

> 'The anthropologist respects history, but he does not accord it a special value. He conceives it as a study complementary to his own: one of them unfurls the range of human societies in time, the other in space. And the difference is even less great than it might seem, since the historian strives to reconstruct the picture of vanished societies as they were at the points which for them corresponded to the present, while the ethnographer does his best to reconstruct the historical stages which temporally preceded their existing form' (S.M.: 256).

Secondly Lévi-Strauss insists that when history takes the form of a recollection of past events it is part of the thinker's present not of his past. For the thinking human being all recollected experience is contemporaneous; as in myth, all events are part of a single synchronous totality. Here the off-stage model is Proust and the penultimate chapter of *La Pensée sauvage* (1962), which is entitled *'Le Temps Retrouvé'*, is plainly intended to echo *'À la Recherche du Temps Perdu'*.

Incidentally the whole corpus of Lévi-Strauss' writings is packed with oblique references and puns of this kind which recall Verlaine's Symbolist formula *'pas de couleur, rien que la nuance'* ('no colour, nothing but nuance'). Davy (1965: 54) has remarked that the Symbolist poets 'insisted that the function of poetic language and particularly of images was not to illustrate ideas but to embody an otherwise indefinable experience'. Readers who find the precise meaning of Lévi-Strauss' prose persistently elusive should remember this part of his literary background.[3]

But on this matter of the Structuralist view of history one further point deserves note. Although Lévi-Strauss constantly reaffirms his view that the structures of primitive thought are present in our modern minds just as much as they are in the minds of those who belong to 'societies without history', he has been very cautious about trying to demonstrate this equivalence. In *La Pensée sauvage*, as we shall see (Chapter 5), he does occasionally consider the application of Structuralist arguments to features of the culture of contemporary Western Europe, but for the most part he draws a sharp (though arbitrary) line between primitive societies, which are grist for the anthropologists because they are timeless and static, and advanced societies, which elude anthropological analysis because they are 'in history'. Lévi-Strauss has consistently refused to apply Structuralist techniques to the analysis of diachronic sequences. Events in the historical past survive in our consciousness only as myth and it is an intrinsic characteristic of myth (and also of Lévi-Strauss' structural analysis) that the chronological sequence of events is irrelevant.[4]

It is in this context that Lévi-Strauss' comments on geology become particularly revealing.

The presuppositions of 19th-century anthropologists were proto-historical, Evolutionist or Diffusionist as the case might be. But Lévi-Strauss' time sense is geological. Although, like Tyler and Frazer, he seems to be interested in the customs of contemporary primitive peoples only because he thinks of them as being in some sense primaeval, he does not argue, as Frazer might have done, that what is primaeval is inferior. In a landscape, rocks of immense antiquity may be found alongside sediments of relatively recent origin, but we do not argue on that account that one is inferior to the other. So also with living things (and by implication human societies):

> 'Sometimes ... on one side and the other of a hidden crevice we find two green plants of different species. Each has chosen the soil which suits it: and we realize that within the rock are two ammonites, one of which has involutions less complex than the other's. We glimpse that is to say a difference of many thousands of years; time and space suddenly commingle; the living diversity of that moment juxtaposes one age and the other and perpetuates them' (W.W.: 60; T.T.E.: 69).

Note that it is not really the green plants that arouse Lévi-Strauss' interest; they merely trigger off his curiosity. His deeper concern is with what is underneath – something altogether more abstract, the relationship between two ammonites, residues of living species which ceased to exist millions of years in the past. And yet again the reason he feels justified in being interested in this abstraction is that it throws light on the present, the difference between his two green plants.

> 'Unlike the history of the historians history as the geologist and the psycho-analyst sees it is intended to body forth in time – rather in the manner of a *tableau vivant* – certain fundamental properties of the physical and psychical universe' (W.W.: 60–1; T.T.E.: 69).

This search for 'fundamental properties' is a recurrent theme in all Lévi-Strauss' writings, but it is not just a matter of antiquarian curiosity. The point is rather that what is fundamental and universal must be the essence of our true nature, and we can use an understanding of that nature to improve ourselves:

> '... the second phase of our undertaking is that while not clinging to elements from any one particular society, we make use of all of them in order to distinguish those principles of social life which may be applied to reform our own customs and not those of customs foreign to our own ... our own society is the only one which we can transform and yet not destroy, since the changes which we should introduce would come from within' (W.W.: 391–2; T.T.E.: 514).

As this passage shows, Lévi-Strauss is a visionary, and the trouble with those who see visions is that they find it very difficult to recognize the plain matter of fact world which the rest of us see all around. Lévi-Strauss pursues his anthropology because he conceives of primitive peoples as 'reduced models' of what is essential in all mankind, but the resulting Rousseau-like noble savages inhabit a world very far removed from the dirt and squalor which is the field anthropologist's normal stamping ground.

This is important. A careful study of *Tristes Tropiques* reveals that, in the whole course of his Brazilian travels, Lévi-Strauss can never have stayed in one place for more than a few weeks at a time and that he was never able to converse easily with any of his native informants in their native language.

There are many kinds of anthropological enquiry, but Malinowski style intensive fieldwork employing the vernacular, which is now the standard research technique employed by nearly all Anglo-American social anthropologists, is an entirely different procedure from the careful but uncomprehending description of manners and customs, based on the use of special informants and interpreters, which was the original source for most of the ethnographic observations on which Lévi-Strauss, like his Frazerian predecessors, has chosen to rely.

It is perfectly true that an experienced anthropologist, visiting a 'new' primitive society for the first time and working with the aid of competent interpreters, may be able, after a stay of only a few days, to develop in his own mind a fairly comprehensive 'model' of how the social system works, but it is also true that if he stays for six months and learns to speak the local language very little of that original 'model' will remain. Indeed the task of understanding how the system works will by then appear even more formidable than it did just two days after his first arrival.

Lévi-Strauss himself has never had the opportunity to suffer this demoralizing experience and he never comes to grips with the issues involved.

In all his writings Lévi-Strauss assumes that the simple, first stage, 'model' generated by the observer's first impressions corresponds quite closely to a genuine (and very important) ethnographic reality – the 'conscious model' which is present in the minds of the anthropologist's informants. In contrast, to anthropologists who have had a wider and more varied range of field experience, it seems all too obvious that this initial model is little more than an amalgam of the observer's own prejudiced presuppositions.

On this account many would argue that Lévi-Strauss, like Frazer, is insufficiently critical of his source material. He always seems to be able to find just what he is looking for. Any evidence however dubious is acceptable so long as it fits with logically calculated expectations; but wherever the data run counter to the theory Lévi-Strauss will either bypass the evidence or marshal the full resources of his power-ful invective to have the heresy thrown out of court! So we need to remember that Lévi-Strauss' prime training was in philosophy and law; he consistently behaves as an advocate defending a cause rather than as a scientist searching for ultimate truth.

But the philosopher-advocate is also a poet. William Empson's *The Seven Types of Ambiguity* (1931) belongs to a class of literary criticism which is wholly antipathetic to contemporary Structuralists, but none the less it makes excellent introductory reading for any would-be student of Lévi-Strauss. Lévi-Strauss has not actually published poetry, but his whole attitude to the sounds and meanings and com-binations and permutations of language elements betrays his nature.

The grand four volume study of the structure of American Indian Mythology is not entitled *Mythologies* but *Mytholo-giques* – the 'logics of myth', and the object of the exercise is to explore the mysterious interconnections between these myth-logics and other logics. This is poet's country and those who get impatient with the tortuous gymnastics of Lévi-Straussian argument – as most of us do – need to remember that he shares with Freud a most remarkable capacity for leading us all unaware into the innermost recesses of our secret emotions.

2 Oysters, Smoked Salmon and Stilton Cheese

Lévi-Strauss is distinguished among the intellectuals of his own country as the leading exponent of 'Structuralism', a word which has come to be used as if it denoted a whole new philosophy of life on the analogy of 'Marxism' or 'Existentialism'. What is this 'Structuralism' all about?

The general argument runs something like this: What we know about the external world we apprehend through our senses. The phenomena which we perceive have the characteristics which we attribute to them because of the way our senses operate and the way the human brain is designed to order and interpret the stimuli which are fed into it. One very important feature of this ordering process is that we cut up the continua of space and time with which we are surrounded into segments so that we are predisposed to think of the environment as consisting of vast numbers of separate things belonging to named classes, and to think of the passage of time as consisting of sequences of separate events. Correspondingly, when, as men, we construct artificial things (artifacts of all kinds), or devise ceremonials, or write histories of the past, we imitate our apprehension of Nature: the products of our Culture are segmented and ordered in the same way as we suppose the products of Nature to be segmented and ordered.

Let me give a very simple example of what I mean. The colour spectrum, which runs from violet, through blue, to green, to yellow, to red, is a continuum. There is no natural point at which green changes to yellow or yellow to red. Our mental recognition of colour is a response to variations in the quality of the light input, notably to luminosity as between dark and light and to wavelength as between long and short. Wavelength gets shorter as we move from infrared to ultra-violet, while temperature, as measured on a thermometer, gets less; luminosity is zero at either end of this spectrum and reaches a maximum in the middle, that is in the yellow.[5] It is a discrimination of the human brain which breaks up this continuum into segments so that we feel that blue, green, yellow, red etc. are quite 'different' colours. This ordering mechanism of the brain is such that anyone who is not colour blind can readily be taught to feel that green is the 'opposite' of red in the same way as black is the opposite of white. In our own culture we have in fact been taught to make this discrimination and because of this we find it appropriate to use red and green signals as if they corresponded to + and –. Actually we make a number of oppositions of this kind in which red is contrasted not only with green but also with other 'colours', notably white, black, blue and yellow. When we make paired oppositions of this kind, red is consistently given the same value, it is treated as a danger sign: hot taps, live electric wires, debit entries in account books, stop signs on roads and railways. This is a pattern which turns up in many other cultures besides our own and in these other cases there is often a quite explicit recognition that the 'danger' of red derives from its 'natural' association with blood.

Anyway, in our case, with traffic lights both on railways and on roads, GREEN means GO and RED means STOP. For many situations this is sufficient. However if we want to devise a further signal with an intermediate meaning – ABOUT TO STOP–ABOUT TO GO, we choose the colour

YELLOW. We do this *because*, in the spectrum, it lies mid-way between GREEN and RED.

In this example the ordering of the colours green–yellow–red is the same as the ordering of the instructions GO–CAUTION–STOP; the colour system and the signal system have the same 'structure', the one is a transformation of the other. But notice how we have arrived at this transformation:

   a. the colour spectrum exists in Nature as a continuum

   b. the human brain interprets this continuum as if it consisted of discontinuous segments

   c. the human brain searches for an appropriate representation of a binary opposition +/– and selects green and red as a binary pair

   d. having set up this polar opposition, the human brain is dissatisfied with the resulting discontinuity and searches for an intermediate position: not +/not –

   e. it then goes back to the original Natural continuum and chooses yellow as the intermediate signal because the brain is able to perceive yellow as a discontinuous intermediate segment lying between green and red

   f. thus the final Cultural product – the three colour traffic signal – is a simplified imitation of a phenomenon of Nature – the colour spectrum – as apprehended by the human brain.

The essence of this whole argument may be exhibited in a diagram which is displayed on the next page (Fig. 1) which represents two superimposed triangles. The corners of the first triangle are the colours GREEN, YELLOW, RED which are differentiated along two axes: (i) short wavelength/long wavelength and (ii) low luminosity/high luminosity. The corners of the second triangle are three instructions concerning movement: GO – continue in a state of movement, CAUTION – prepare to change your state of movement, STOP – continue in a state of non-movement. These messages are again differentiated along two axes: (i) movement/no movement and (ii) change/no change. By superimposing one schema on the other the colours become signals for the underlying instructions: the natural structure of the colour relations is the same as the logical structure relating the three instructions:

FIG. I   *Traffic signal colour triangle*

This particular example has not, so far as I am aware, ever been used by Lévi-Strauss, but the Structuralist thesis is that triangles of this kind, implying comparable transformations of models of Nature as apprehended by human brains, have very general application, though, in the general case, the possibilities are more complicated.

In my example, the pattern was subject to two special constraints: firstly it is a 'fact of Nature' that the sequence of colours in the spectrum is green–yellow–red and not yellow–green–red or green–red–yellow, and secondly there is the further fact of Nature, which certainly goes back to

very early palaeolithic times, that human beings have a tendency to make a direct association between *red* as a colour
and *blood* as a substance, so that, if any one of these three
colours is to be selected to mean: 'stop – danger', it is much
more likely to be *red* than either *yellow* or *green*. On this
account the correlation between the members of the two
triads are, in this case, more or less pre-determined. The

equivalences: $\begin{cases} \text{red--yellow--green} \\ \text{STOP--CAUTION--GO} \end{cases}$

are given and we do not need to pay attention to alternative
possibilities offered by the rest of the matrix:

	Stop	Caution	Go
actual sequence	red	yellow	green
other possible	red	green	yellow
sequences	yellow	red	green
	yellow	green	red
	green	yellow	red
	green	red	yellow

But in the general case, a structural analysis needs to start
by setting out *all* the possible permutations and to proceed
by examination of the empirical evidence on a comparative
basis. Lévi-Strauss himself puts it this way:

'The method we adopt, ... consists of the following
operations:

i. define the phenomenon under study as a relation
between two or more terms, real or supposed:

ii. construct a table of possible permutations between these terms;

iii. take this table as the general object of analysis which, at this level only, can yield necessary connections, the empirical phenomenon considered at the beginning being only one possible combination among others, the complete system of which must be constructed beforehand' (T.: 16).

As I have explained for the traffic signal case, the ultimate object of the exercise is to discover how relations which exist in Nature (and are apprehended as such by human brains) are used to generate cultural products which incorporate these same relations. This point must not be misunderstood. Lévi-Strauss is not an idealist in the style of Bishop Berkeley; he is not arguing that Nature has no existence other than in its apprehension by human minds. Lévi-Strauss' Nature is a genuine reality 'out there'; it is governed by natural laws which are accessible, at least in part, to human scientific investigation but our capacity to apprehend the nature of Nature is severely restricted by the nature of the apparatus through which we do the apprehending. Lévi-Strauss' thesis is that by noticing *how* we apprehend Nature, by observing the qualities of the classifications which we use and the way we manipulate the resulting categories, we shall be able to infer crucial facts about the mechanism of thinking.

After all, since human brains are themselves natural objects and since they are substantially the same throughout the species *Homo sapiens*, we must suppose that when cultural products are generated in the way I have described the process must impart to them certain universal (natural) characteristics of the brain itself. Thus, in investigating the elementary structures of cultural phenomena, we are also making discoveries about the nature of Man – facts which are true of you and me as well as of the naked savages of Central Brazil. Lévi-Strauss puts it this way:

> 'Anthropology affords me an intellectual satisfaction: it rejoins at one extreme the history of the world and at the other the history of myself, and it unveils the shared motivation of one and the other at the same moment' (W.W.: 62; T.T.E.: 72).

It is important to understand just what is being proposed. In a superficial sense the products of culture are enormously varied and when an anthropologist sets out to compare, let us say, the culture of the Australian Aborigines with that of the Eskimo or that of the English he is first of all impressed by the differences. Yet since all cultures are the product of human brains, there must be, somewhere beneath the surface, features that are common to all.

This, in itself, is no new idea. A much older generation of anthropologists, notably Bastian (1826–1905) in Germany and Frazer (1854–1941) in England held that because all men belong to one species there must be psychological universals (*Elementargedanken*) which should manifest themselves in the occurrence of similar customs among peoples 'who had reached the same stage of evolutionary development' all over the world. Frazer and his contemporaries assiduously compiled immense catalogues of 'similar' customs which were designed to exhibit this evolutionary principle. This is *not* what the Structuralists are up to. The recurrence of a detail of custom in two different parts of the map is not a matter to which Lévi-Strauss attaches any particular importance. In his view, the universals of human culture exist only at the level of structure never at the level of manifest fact. We may usefully compare the patterning of the relations which links together sets of human behaviours, but we shall *not* learn anything if we simply compare single cultural items as isolates. In the traffic signal case, it is the contrast between the colours and the switching from one colour to another that provides the information; each colour has relevance only in relation to the others.

These very general ideas are a development of arguments originally developed by the Prague school of structural linguists but particularly by Roman Jakobson, who spent the last four decades of his life in the United States and who was an academic colleague of Lévi-Strauss at the New School for Social Research in New York at the end of the last war. The influence on Lévi-Strauss of Jakobson's style of phonemic analysis, which derives in turn from much earlier work of de Saussure, has been very marked. Lévi-Strauss repeatedly makes an assumption that other modes of cultural expression, such as kinship systems and folk taxonomies, are organized like human language. This culture/language analogy has been developed out of Jakobson's distinctive feature theory and Lévi-Strauss has not exploited the additional insights which might have been derived from Chomsky's thinking about generative grammars. Incidentally Chomsky himself has expressly declared that Lévi-Strauss' use of linguistic analogies is unjustified (Chomsky 1968: 65), though he agrees that Jakobson's argument must constitute a basic part of any general linguistic theory, including his own (Chomsky 1964: 67).[6]

It is interesting to see how Lévi-Strauss sets about deriving his cultural generalizations from his linguistic base. His discussion of the 'culinary triangle' provides a case in point. This is one of the major themes which persists throughout the *Mythologiques* series but it has also been the subject of an independent article which I will summarize here (see T.C., 1965).

Lévi-Strauss begins with a brief reference to Jakobson's thesis in the following terms:

> 'In all the languages of the world the complex systems of oppositions between the phonemes are no more than a multi-directional elaboration of a more simple system which is common to all, namely the contrast between consonant and vowel, which through the working of a double opposition between compact and diffuse, acute and grave, generates on the one hand what we may call the "vocalic triangle":

> and on the other the "consonant triangle"':

Most readers are likely to find such a pronouncement somewhat baffling, so I will give a rather more extended version of the original doctrine.

Jakobson claims that young children gain control of the basic vowels and consonants so as to generate meaningful noise patterns in a standardized sequence (see Jakobson and

Halle, 1956: 38f.). The child first develops the basic vowel/
consonant opposition by discriminating a contrast in
loudness:

Vowel (V)	Consonant (C)
(high energy noise)	(low energy noise)
(loud-compact)	(soft-diffuse)

The undifferentiated consonant (C) is then split by discriminating pitch – a low frequency (grave) component ('p') and
a high frequency (acute) component ('t'). The high energy
(compact) velar stop consonant ('k') then complements the
undifferentiated high energy (compact) vowel ('a') while the
low energy (diffuse) consonants ('p', 't') are complemented
by corresponding low energy (diffuse) vowels ('u'-grave,
'i'-acute).

The whole argument may be represented by a double
triangle of consonants and vowels (Fig. 2) discriminated as
compact/diffuse, and grave/acute.

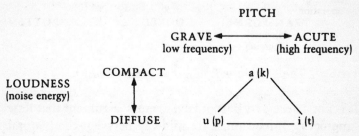

FIG. 2 *Jakobson's Primary Vowel-Consonant Triangles*

But let me go back to the 'Culinary Triangle'. After his
initial brief reference to the linguistic prototype, Lévi-
Strauss observes that just as there is no human society
which lacks a spoken language so also there is no human

society which does not, in one way or another, process some of its food supply by cooking. But cooked food may be thought of as fresh raw food which has been transformed (*élaboré*) by cultural means, whereas rotten food is fresh raw food which has been transformed by natural means. Thus, just as Jakobson's vowel-consonant triangles, represent the binary oppositions compact/diffuse and grave/acute which have become internalized into the child's computer-like mental processes, so also we can construct a culinary triangle to represent the binary oppositions: transformed/normal and Culture/Nature which are (by implication) internalized into the *eidos* of human culture everywhere.[7]

FIG. 3   *The Culinary Triangle (Primary Form)*

It is not a necessary part of Lévi-Strauss' argument that Raw (unprocessed) food must lie midway between the Natural and the Cultural, though it is of course a fact that most unprocessed human foodstuffs fall into the category 'domesticated plants and animals', i.e. they *are* both cultural and natural.

Finally Lévi-Strauss completes his exercise in intellectual gymnastics by claiming that the principal modes of cooking form another structured set which is the converse of the first:

i. *Roasting* is a process in which the meat is brought into direct contact with the agent of conversion (fire) without the mediation of any cultural apparatus or of air or of water; the process is only partial – roast meat is only partly cooked.

ii. *Boiling* is a process which reduces the raw food to a decomposed state similar to natural rotting, but it requires the mediation of both water and a receptacle – an object of Culture.

iii. *Smoking* is a process of slow but complete cooking; it is accomplished without the mediation of any cultural apparatus, but with the mediation of air.

Thus, as to means, roasting and smoking are natural processes whereas boiling is a cultural process, but, as to end-products, smoked food belongs to Culture but roast and boiled food to Nature.

Lévi-Strauss summarizes his whole argument in the following diagram:

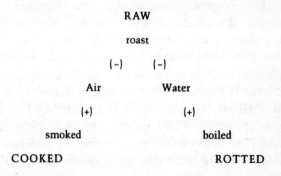

FIG. 4   *The Culinary Triangle (Developed Form)*

In his original article (T.C.: 1965) Lévi-Strauss qualifies the generality of this schema by noting that our own system, which distinguishes *grilling* from *roasting*, and *steaming* from *boiling* and adds a category *frying* (which is a form of boiling in which oil is substituted for water), requires a much more complicated model – and at this point some English readers might begin to suspect that the whole argument was an elaborate academic joke. But exactly the same diagram (Fig. 4) appears in *Mythologiques* III (O.M.: 406; O.T.M.: 490) accompanied by the same text, so we must try to take the matter seriously. But this is rather difficult. Lévi-Strauss has not adhered to his own rules of procedure as specified above (p. 34) and the whole operation suggests a game of acrostics in which appropriate words have been slipped into the vacant slots of a prearranged verbal matrix. Elsewhere Lévi-Strauss has claimed that 'behind all sense there is a non-sense' (R. 1963: 637) but perhaps the best that one could claim for this fandangle is that 'behind the nonsense there is a sense' even if it is not the sense of ordinary conversation.

What Lévi-Strauss is getting at is this. *Animals* just eat food; and food is anything which is available which their instincts place in the category 'edible'. But *human beings*, once they have been weaned from the mother's breast, have no such instincts. It is the conventions of society which decree what is food and what is not food, and what kinds of food shall be eaten on what occasions. And since the occasions are social occasions there must be some kind of patterned homology between relationships between kinds of food on the one hand and relationships between social occasions on the other.

Moreover, when we look into the facts, the categories which are treated as significant *kinds* of food become interesting in themselves. The diet of any particular human population is dependent upon the availability of resources and, at the level of actual items of foodstuff (bread, mutton, cheese and so on), there is very little overlap between the shopping list of an English housewife and the inventory of comestibles available to an Amazonian Indian. But the English housewife and the Amazonian Indian alike break up the unitary category 'food' into a number of sub-categories, 'food A', 'food B', 'food C', etc., each of which is treated in a different way. But, at *this* level, the categories A, B, C, etc., turn out to be remarkably alike everywhere. They are in fact categories of the kind which appear in Fig. 4, and the significant thing about such categories is that they are accorded very different levels of social prestige. I do not mean only that the different components of the feast can always be fitted into our prearranged slots: Oysters (raw), Smoked Salmon (smoked), Lobster Soup (boiled), Saddle of Mutton (roast), Soufflé (cooked), Stilton Cheese (rotted) – but rather that foods of these different general classes bear a standardized relationship to each other. For example, according to our conventions, whenever the menu includes a dish of roast meat it will be accorded pride of place in the middle; steamed and boiled foods on the other hand are considered especially suitable for invalids and children. Why should this be? Why should we tend to think of boiled fowl as a homely dish, but roast chicken as a party dish?

All sorts of rationalizations can be devised to fit any particular case, for example that boiling fowls are cheaper than roasters, or that boiled food is 'more digestible' (What is the evidence for this?), but all such explanations begin to look rather thin once it is realized that other peoples, with very different cultures from our own, sort out their foodstuffs in very similar ways, and apply status distinctions of comparable sort. Some foods are appropriate only to men, others only to women: some foods are forbidden to children, some can only be eaten on ceremonial occasions. The resulting pattern is not always the same, but it is certainly very far from random – Lévi-Strauss has even claimed that the high status which attaches to roasting as against boiling is a *universal* cultural characteristic, so that boiled food is only highly regarded in relatively democratic types of society: 'Boiling provides a means of complete conservation of the meat and its juices, whereas roasting is accompanied by destruction and loss. Thus one denotes economy; the other prodigality; the latter is aristocratic, the former plebeian'! (T.C.: 23).

An odd line of thought certainly, yet if we accept Lévi-Strauss' unexpected frame of reference, such comments are nothing like so arbitrary as they may appear. In that we are men, we are all a part of Nature; in that we are human beings, we are all a part of Culture. Our survival as men depends on our ingestion of food (which is a part of Nature); our survival as human beings depends upon our use of social categories which are derived from cultural classifications imposed on elements of Nature. The social use of categories of food is thus homologous with the social use of categories of colour in the traffic signal case (p. 32). But food is an especially appropriate 'mediator' because, when we eat, we establish, in a literal sense, a direct identity between ourselves (Culture) and our food (Nature). Cooking is thus universally a means by which Nature is transformed into Culture, and categories of cooking are always peculiarly appropriate for use as symbols of social differentiation.

In another context where Lévi-Strauss is concerned to debunk the anthropological mystique which has clustered around the concept of Totemism, he has criticized the functionalist thesis that totemic species are given social value because they are of economic value. On the contrary says Lévi-Strauss it is the species themselves considered simply as categories which are socially valuable: totemic species are 'goods to think with' (*bonnes à penser*) rather than 'goods to eat' (*bonnes à manger*). All this stuff about the culinary triangle is the other side of the same argument. Foodstuffs, as such, are of course 'goods to eat'; but this alone does not explain the complications which we inject into the classification of food; food *species* like totemic *species* are 'goods to think with' (cf. pp. 51–54 below).[8]

This is an unfamiliar style of discourse and it has to be admitted that here as elsewhere in Lévi-Strauss' writings there is an element of verbal sleight of hand which invites caution rather than enthusiasm. All the same the reader should not imagine that the 'culinary triangle' is just an elegant *jeu d'esprit* by a master of the unexpected analogy. Lévi-Strauss has by now marshalled a great deal of evidence to show that the process of food preparation and the categories of food with which they are associated are everywhere elaborately structured and that there are universal principles underlying these structures. Moreover the method of analysis however bizarre it may appear, has wide application. The culinary triangle first appeared in print only in 1965 but triangles of comparable type feature in many earlier parts of the Lévi-Straussian corpus.

In the 1945 paper which is the foundation work for all his subsequent structural anthropology (see S.A. Chapter 2) the corners of the triangle are MUTUALITY, RIGHTS, OBLIGATIONS while the binary oppositions appear to be: exchange/no exchange and receivers/givers. In S.E.P. (1945: 575; or see E.S.K.:465): the triangle becomes: BILATERAL MARRIAGE, PATRILATERAL CROSS-COUSIN MARRIAGE,

MATRILATERAL CROSS-COUSIN MARRIAGE, and the oppositions symmetry/asymmetry alternation/repetition. G.A. (1960) includes a highly complicated triangle which combines geographical and food category parameters in such a way that vegetable food is opposed to animal food, sea to land, East to West, and definition to lack of definition. This is not just a game. Lévi-Strauss is endeavouring to establish the rudiments of a semantic algebra. If cultural behaviour is capable of conveying information then the code in which cultural messages are expressed must have an algebraic structure. It is possible that Lévi-Strauss is making larger claims for the importance of this algebra than is justified by the evidence, but there is more to it than a trickster's game of noughts and crosses. Let us go back to the beginning.

3   The Human Animal and his Symbols

Lévi-Strauss' central intellectual puzzle is one to which European philosophers have returned over and over again; indeed if we accept Lévi-Strauss' own view of the matter it is a problem which puzzles all mankind, everywhere, always. Quite simply: What is Man? Man is an animal, a member of the species *Homo sapiens*, closely related to the great Apes and more distantly to all other living species past and present. But Man, we assert, is a human being, and in saying that we evidently mean that he is, in some way, other than 'just an animal'. But in what way is he other? The concept of humanity as distinct from animality does not readily translate into exotic languages but it is Lévi-Strauss' thesis that a distinction of this sort – corresponding to the opposition Culture/Nature – is always latent in men's customary attitudes and behaviours even when it is not explicitly formulated in words. The human Ego is never by himself, there is no 'I' that is not part of a 'We',[9] and indeed every 'I' is a member of many 'We's'. In one sense these we-groups stretch out to infinity in all directions to embrace everybody and everything ... 'Man is not alone in the universe, any more than the individual is alone in the group, or any one society alone among other societies' (W.W.: 398; T.T.E.: 544), but in practice we cut up the continua. My particular 'we', the people of *my* family, *my* community, *my* tribe, *my* class ... these are altogether special, they are superior, they are civilized, cultured, the others are just savages, like wild beasts.

Lévi-Strauss' central preoccupation is to explore the dialectical process by which this apotheosis of ourselves as human and godlike and other than animal is formed and reformed and bent back upon itself. Adam and Eve were created as ignorant savages in Paradise in a world in which animals talked and were helpmeets to Man; it was through sin that they gained knowledge and became human, and different, and superior to the animals. But are we really 'superior'? God made Man in his own image, but are we so sure that in achieving humanity (Culture) we did not separate ourselves from God? This is the note on which Lévi-Strauss ends *Tristes Tropiques* the book which first brought him international renown outside the narrow world of professional anthropology: to discover the nature of Man we must find our way back to an understanding of how Man is related to Nature, and he comes back to the same theme in the closing paragraph of the third volume of *Mythologiques*. We (Europeans), he comments, have been taught from infancy to be self centred and individualistic 'to fear the impurity of foreign things', a doctrine which we embody in the formula 'Hell is the others' (*l'enfer, c'est les autres*) but primitive myth has the opposite moral implication 'Hell is ourselves' (*l'enfer, c'est nous-même*)[10] 'In a century when man is bent on the destruction of innumerable forms of life' it is necessary to insist, as in the myths, 'that a properly appointed humanism cannot begin of its own accord but must place the world before life, life before man, and the respect of others before self-interest' (O.M.: 422; O.T.M.: 508). But, the puzzle remains, what is a human being? Where does Culture divide off from Nature?

Lévi-Strauss himself takes his cue from Rousseau, though

he might equally well have followed Vico or Hobbes or
Aristotle or a dozen others. It is a language which makes
Man different:

> *Qui dit homme, dit langage, et qui dit langage dit société*
> (T.T.: 421; T.T.E.: 551).

But the emergence of language which accompanies the shift
from animality to humanity, from nature to culture, is also
a shift from affectivity to a state of reasoning, 'the first
speech was all in poetry; reasoning was thought of only long
afterwards' (Rousseau, 1783: 565).

Rousseau's thesis, as elaborated by Lévi-Strauss, is that
Man can only become self-conscious – aware of himself as
a member of a we-group – when he becomes capable of
employing metaphor of an instrument of contrast and comparison:

> 'It is only because man originally felt himself identical
> to all those like him (among which, as Rousseau explicitly
> says, we must include animals) that he came to acquire
> the capacity to distinguish *himself* as he distinguishes
> *them*, i.e. to use the diversity of species as conceptual
> support for social differentiation' (T.: 101).

Rousseau's insight can only be held to be 'true' in a strictly
poetic sense, for the thought processes of proto-man are even
less accessible to us than those of apes and monkeys. But
the philogenetic form of argument is mixed up with Lévi-
Strauss' search for human universals: verbal categories provide the mechanism through which *universal* structural
characteristics of human brains are transformed into *universal* structural characteristics of human culture. But if these
universals exist, they must, at some rather deep level, be
considered innate. In that case, we must suppose that they

49

are patterns which, in the course of human evolution, have become internalized into the human psyche along with the specialized development of those parts of the human brain which are directly concerned with speech formation through the larynx and mouth and speech reception through the ear. And why not? After all, although the human infant is not born with any innate language, it *is* born with an innate capacity both to learn how to make meaningful utterances and also how to decode the meaningful utterances of others.

Not only that but, if Jakobson's argument is correct, all human children will learn to master the basic elements of their phonemic inventory by making the same, or very nearly the same, initial series of basic discriminations: consonant/vowel, nasal consonant/oral stop, grave/acute, compact/diffuse ... They presumably do this not so much because of any instinct but because the architecture of the human mouth and throat and its associated musculature makes this the *natural* way to go about it. Lévi-Strauss asks us to believe that category formation in human beings follow similar universal natural paths. It is not that it *must* always happen the same way everywhere but that the human brain is so constructed that it is predisposed to develop categories of a particular kind in a particular way.[11]

All animals have a certain limited capacity to make category distinctions. Any mammal or bird can, under appropriate conditions, recognize other members of its own species and distinguish males from females; some can further recognize a category of predator enemies. Human beings, in the process of learning to talk, extend this category-forming capacity to a degree that has no parallel among other creatures, but nevertheless, at its very roots, before the individual's language capacity has become elaborated, category formation must be animal-like rather than human-like. At this basic level the individual (whether animal or human) is concerned only with very simple problems: the distinction between own species and other, dominance and submission, sexual availability or lack of availability, what is edible and what is not. In a natural environment distinctions of this sort are all that are necessary for individual survival, but they are *not* sufficient within a human environment. For human (as distinct from animal) survival every member of society must learn to distinguish his fellow men according to their mutual social status. But the simplest way to do this is to apply transformations of the animal level categories to the social classification of human beings. This is the key point in Lévi-Strauss' Structuralist approach to the classic anthropological theme of Totemism.

It is a fact of empirical observation that human beings everywhere adopt ritual attitudes towards the animals and plants in their vicinity. Consider, for example, the separate, and often bizarre, rules which govern the behaviour of Englishmen towards the creatures which they classify as: (i) wild animals, (ii) foxes, (iii) game, (iv) farm animals, (v) pets, (vi) vermin. Notice further that if we take the sequence of words: (ia) strangers, (iia) enemies, (iiia) friends, (iva) neighbours, (va) companions, (via) criminals, the two sets of terms are in some degree homologous. By a metaphorical usage the categories of animals could be (and sometimes are) used as equivalents for the categories of human beings. One of Lévi-Strauss' major contributions to our understanding has been to show how very widespread is this kind of socialization of animal categories. The facts themselves are well known but, in Lévi-Strauss' view, they have been misunderstood.

The conventions by which primitive peoples use species of plants and animals as symbols for categories of men are not really any more eccentric than our own but, in a techno-logically restricted environment, they become much more noticeable and to scholars of Sir James Frazer's generation they seemed altogether extraordinary. So much so that any social equivalence between human beings and other natural species came to be regarded as a kind of cult (totemism) – a proto-religion appropriate only to people at a very early stage of development. It was recognized right from the start that elements of 'totemic' behaviour occur even in sophisti-cated cultures, but the earlier writers interpreted these details as archaic residues which had somehow survived into our own day from the remote past. In the more general primitive case 'totemism' was thought to pose a basic prob-lem of rationality.

Why should sane human beings indulge in the 'super-stitious worship' of animals and plants? How can men come to imagine that they are descended from kangaroos, or wal-labies, or white cockatoos? A great variety of possible answers to such questions were proposed. Van Gennep (1920) was able to distinguish 41 different 'theories of totem-ism' and more have accumulated since then. Broadly speak-ing they fall into two types:

i. Universalist explanations implying that totemic beliefs and practices indicate a 'childish' mentality which had once been characteristic of all mankind.

ii. Particularist explanations resting on the functionalist proposition that any totemic system will serve to attach emotional interest to animal and plant species which are of economic value to the particular human society concerned and will thereby tend to preserve those species from total destruction by human depredation.

After the publication of Goldenweiser (1910) theories of the first kind were barely tenable and thereafter, down to

1962, the more worthwhile contributions to the subject were concerned with particular ethnographies – Australia, Tikopia, Tallensi – rather than with universal truth. But Radcliffe-Brown (1929) is a special case because it attempts to generalize the functionalist position; 'totemism' is here treated as a near-universal and is seen as the ritual expression of interdependence between social order and the natural environment. In a later essay Radcliffe-Brown (1951) carried this universalist thesis a good deal further, drawing special attention to the classificatory nature of ethnic systems. Some features of this latter paper are so markedly 'Structuralist' in style that it provided the trigger for Lévi-Strauss' own contribution, *Le Totemisme aujourd'hui* (1962) [*Totemism* (1964)].

Lévi-Strauss takes the view that the anthropologists who have tried to isolate 'totemism' as a phenomenon *sui generis* have deluded themselves; considered as a religious system 'totemism' is an anthropological mirage; even so, the subject deserves our close attention because totemic beliefs and practices exemplify a universal characteristic of human thought.

Lévi-Strauss' account does not add anything of significance to our understanding of Australian totemism, but his re-appraisal of Radcliffe-Brown's arguments makes it much easier to understand how the seemingly bizarre thought categories of the Australian aborigines are related to category systems with which we are more familiar. The crux of his argument is that totemic systems always embody metaphoric systems of the sort indicated above (p. 51). This metaphor formation is discussed in greater detail later in this chapter (pp. 58–61). Incidentally it was with reference to 'totemism' that Lévi-Strauss came up with his own summary of what constitutes the essence of structuralist method which I have quoted already at pp. 34–5. Note in particular his seeming contempt for the 'empirical phenomenon'. The 'general object of analysis' is conceived as a kind of algebraic matrix of possible permutations and combinations located in the unconscious 'human mind'; the empirical evidence is merely an example of what is possible. This same preference for the generalized abstraction as compared with the empirical fact occurs again and again throughout Lévi-Strauss writings. Mind you, that is not how Lévi-Strauss himself sees the situation. He conceives of 'the human mind' as having objective existence; it is an attribute of human brains. We can ascertain attributes of this human mind by investigating and comparing its cultural products. The study of 'empirical phenomena' is thus an essential part of the process of discovery but it is only a means to an end.[12]

But let us go back to Rousseau's vision of Man as a talking animal. Until a few years ago it was customary for anthropologists to draw a very sharp distinction between Culture, which was conceived of as exclusively human, and Nature, which was common to all animals, including man. This distinction, according to Leslie White:

> 'is one of kind not of degree. And the gap between the two types is of the greatest importance . . . Man uses symbols; no other creature does. An organism has the ability to symbol or it does not, there are no intermediate stages' (White, 1949: 25).

In his earlier writings, though less emphatically in his later ones, Lévi-Strauss reiterates this view. The special marker of symbolic thought is the existence of spoken language in which words stand for (signify) things 'out there' which are signified. Signs must be distinguished from triggers. Animals of all kinds respond mechanically to appropriate signals; this process does *not* entail 'symbolic thought'. In order to be able to operate with symbols it is necessary first of all to be able to distinguish between the sign and the thing it signifies and then to be able to recognize that there is a relation between the sign and the thing signified. This is the cardinal characteristic which distinguishes human thought from animal response – the ability to distinguish A from B while at the same time recognizing that A and B are somehow interdependent.

This distinction can be put in another way. When an individual acts as an individual, operating upon the world outside himself – e.g. if he uses a spade to dig a hole in the ground – he is *not* concerned with symbolization, but the moment some other individual comes onto the scene *every* action, however trivial, serves to communicate information about the actor to the observer – the observed details are interpreted as signs, because observer and actor are in relation. From this point of view the animals in any human environment serve as things with which to think (*bonnes à penser*).[13]

When Lévi-Strauss poses for himself the seemingly quite unanswerable puzzle of how should this faculty for symbolic interpretation come into being, he finds his answer in an adaptation of ideas borrowed from Durkheim and his immediate pupils. Certain binary concepts are part of man's nature – e.g. men and women are alike in one sense yet opposite and interdependent in another; the right hand and the left hand are, likewise, equal and opposite yet related. In society, as it actually exists, we find that such natural pairs are invariably loaded with cultural significance – they are made into the prototype symbols of the good and the bad, the permitted and the forbidden. Furthermore, in society as it actually exists, individuals are social persons who are 'in relation' to one another, e.g. as father to son or as employer to employee. These individuals communicate with one another by 'exchange'; they exchange words, they exchange gifts. These words and gifts communicate information because they are signs, not because they are things in themselves. When an employer pays out wages to an employee, the action *signifies* the relative status of the parties to the transaction. But, according to Lévi-Strauss (if I understand him correctly), the ultimate basic symbolic exchange which provides the model for all the others is sexual. The incest taboo (which Lévi-Strauss erroneously claims to be 'universal') implies a capacity to distinguish between women who are permitted and women who are forbidden and thus generates a distinction between women of the category *wife* and women of the category *sister*. The *basis* of human exchange, and hence the basis of symbolic thought and the beginning of culture, lies in the uniquely human phenomenon that a man is able to establish a relationship with another man by means of an exchange of women. I shall come back to this again in Chapter 6.

But let me take up once more my earlier point that Lévi-Strauss seems to be more interested in an algebra of possibilities than in the empirical facts. His justification is this. In actual social life individuals are communicating with one another all the time by elaborate combinations of signs – by words, by the clothes they wear, by the food they eat, by the way they stand, by the way they arrange the furniture of a room and so on. In any particular case there will be a certain discoverable consistency between behaviours at these different levels; e.g. in England, members of the upper middle class living in Kensington will adopt for each of the 'codes' I have mentioned, quite a different style from members of, say, the working class in Leeds. But any particular empirical case is only one alternative from a whole set of possibilities, and, according to Lévi-Strauss and his followers, we shall gain additional insight into the empirical cases which we *have* observed by considering their relationship to the possible cases which we have *not* observed.

At this point it is necessary to make something of a digression. Lévi-Strauss' ideas about how human beings are able to communicate through symbols are a development from arguments originally developed by specialists in structural linguistics and semiology (the theory of signs). But the latter have used a very varied and confusing terminology and it may help if I try to sort out some of the equivalents.

The first basic distinction is that of de Saussure between language (*langue*) and speech (*parole*). 'The English language' denotes a total system of word conventions and usages; from the point of view of any particular individual speaker it is a 'given', it is not something he creates for himself; the parts of the language are available for us, but they do not have to be used. But when I, as an individual, make an utterance I use 'speech'; I select from the total system of 'the language' certain words and grammatical conventions and tones and accents, and by placing these in a particular *order* I am able to transmit information by my utterance.

There is a close, but not exact, equivalence between the distinction *language* and *speech*, as specified above, and the information theory distinction between *code* and *message*. If we, in fact, think of a spoken language as a code, then it is a particular kind of code – namely it is a code made up of sound elements. But there are many other kinds of possible codes. As I suggested just now, we use clothes as a code, or kinds of food, or gestures, or postures, and so on. Each such code is 'a language' (in de Saussure's sense) and the sum of all such codes i.e. the Culture of the individual actor is also 'a language'.

Now the verbal boxes which I have used in this argument, e.g. 'sound elements', 'clothes', 'kinds of food' etc., lump things together because they are associated in our minds as somehow similar in function or 'meaning', whereas when I make a verbal utterance and transmit a message – 'the cat sat on the mat' – the elements are brought together in a chain as a result of the rules of the language and not because they are in any way similar in themselves. This is what I mean when I refer later to 'syntagmatic chains' – they are chains formed by the application of rules of syntax.

In the same way, we need to distinguish the mental associ-ation which tells us that roast turkey and boiled chicken are both 'kinds of food' (and therefore parts of one language) from the rules of particular languages (cultures) which may specify, for example, that in England roast beef should be eaten in association with Yorkshire pudding or, to be more complex, that a menu consisting of roast turkey followed by flaming plum pudding and mince pies probably indicates that it is December 25th.

Many readers are likely to find this use of the word 'language' to refer to non-verbal forms of communication somewhat confusing and matters are not made any easier by the fact that Barthes (1967), who presents the general Structuralist argument with relative clarity, uses yet another terminology. On p. 59 I give a modified version of a table which Barthes employs to explain the relationship between metaphoric (paradigmatic) and metonymic (syntag-matic) uses of non-verbal signs. In the original Barthes uses the term *system* in two different senses, firstly to denote what I have referred to above as 'a language' and secondly to denote the 'parts of speech' of such a language,

Syntagm and System

(from Barthes 1967: 63. [The words in square brackets have been added].)

	[A]	[B]
	System [Parts of speech: nouns, verbs, etc.]	*Syntagm* [Sentence.]
Garment 'system' [language] [code]	Set of pieces, parts or details which cannot be worn at the same time on the same part of the body, and whose variation corresponds to a change in the meaning of the clothing: toque – bonnet – hood, etc.	Juxtaposition in the same type of dress of different elements: skirt – blouse – jacket.
Food 'system' [language] [code]	Set of foodstuffs which have affinities or differences, within which one chooses a dish in view of a certain meaning: the types of entree, roast or sweet.	Real sequence of dishes chosen during a meal: this is the menu.
	A restaurant 'menu' actualizes both planes: the horizontal reading of the entrees, for instance, corresponds to the system, the vertical reading of the menu corresponds to the syntagm.	
Furniture 'system' [language] [code]	Set of 'stylistic' varieties of a single piece of furniture (a bed).	Juxtaposition of the different pieces of furniture in the same space: bed – wardrobe – table, etc.
Architecture 'system' [language] [code]	Variations in style of a single element in a building, various types of roof, balcony, hall, etc.	Sequence of the details at the level of the whole building.

i.e. the sets of objects which correspond to the sets of words which, in a verbal language, we would distinguish as 'nouns', 'verbs', 'adjectives', etc. I have modified this diagram by writing the first of these usages *'system'* and the second *system*. In this schema the term *syntagm*, as applied to an assemblage of non-verbal signs, corresponds to *sentence* in a verbal language.

The distinction between the Columns A and B in this diagram is very important for any understanding of Lévi-Strauss' writings but he himself does not use this terminology. Where Barthes opposes *system* and *syntagm*, the corresponding contrasts in Lévi-Strauss are *metaphor* and *metonymy* or sometimes *paradigmatic series* and *syntagmatic chain* (see e.g. p. 108 below). Although the jargon is exasperating the principles are simple. As Jakobson put it, metaphor (system, paradigm) relies on the recognition of similarity and metonymy (syntagm) on the recognition of contiguity (Jakobson and Halle, 1956: 81).

Lévi-Strauss maintains that in the analysis of myth and of primitive thought generally, we need to distinguish between these two poles. For example, if we imagine another world peopled by supernatural beings then we can represent this other world in any number of ways: as a society of birds, or of fishes, or of wild animals, or even of beings 'like' men, and in each case we shall be using *metaphor*. That is one kind of symbolization. But there is also another kind in which we rely on the fact that our audience, being aware of how a particular syntagm (sentence) is formed out of the elements of the 'system' (language, code), is able to recognize the whole by being shown only a part. This is *metonymy*. For example, when we use the formula 'the Crown stands for Sovereignty' we are relying on the fact that a crown is uniquely associated with a particular syntagmatic chain of items of clothing which together form the uniform of a particular office holder, the King, so that, even when removed from this context of proper use, it can still be used as a signifier for the whole complex. This metaphor/metonymy opposition is not an either/or distinction; there is always some element of both kinds of association in any communicative discourse but there can be marked differences of emphasis. As I have said, 'The Crown stands for Sovereignty' is primarily metonymic; in contrast, the concept of a 'queen bee' is metaphoric.

All this links up with a much earlier style of anthropological analysis. Frazer started his classic study of primitive magic (*The Golden Bough*, Abridged Edn.: 12) with the thesis that magical beliefs depend on two types of (erroneous) mental association: homeopathic magic, depending on a law of similarity, and contagious magic, depending on a law of contact. Frazer's homeopathic/contagious distinction is practically identical to the Jakobson–Lévi-Strauss metaphoric/metonymic distinction, and the fact that Frazer and Lévi-Strauss should both agree that this kind of discrimination is highly relevant for an understanding of 'primitive thought' seems very significant.

But how does all this tie in with Lévi-Strauss' general attitude to the process of symbolization?

Well first of all it needs to be appreciated that these two dimensions – the metaphoric-paradigmatic-harmonic-similarity axis on the one hand and the metonymic-syntagmatic-melodic-contagious axis on the other – correspond to the logical framework within which the various structural triangles of Chapter 2 are constructed. For example, if we take Fig. 3 (p. 40), the Culture/Nature axis is 'metaphoric' while the normal/transformed axis is 'metonymic'. But it is more immediately relevant in the present context that, for Lévi-Strauss, this same framework provides the clue for our understanding of totemism and myth. Considered as individual items of culture a totemic ritual or a myth is syntagmatic – it consists of a sequence of details linked together in a chain; animals and men are apparently interchangeable, Culture and Nature are confused. But if we take a whole set of such rituals and myths and superimpose one upon another, then a paradigmatic-metaphoric pattern is seen to emerge – it becomes apparent that the variations of what happens to the animals are algebraic transformations of the variations of what happens to the men, as in the example on p. 51.

Alternatively we can operate the other way round. If we start with a particular sequence of customary behaviour we should regard it as a syntagm, a special case of ordered relations among a set of cultural oddments which, in itself, is just a residue of history. If we take such a special case and consider the arrangements between its component parts algebraically we can arrive at the total system, a theme and variations, – a set of paradigms (metaphors) of which our special case is just one example. This will bring to our attention all sorts of other possible variations and we can then take another look at our ethnographic data to see if these other variations actually occur. If they do then we shall have confirmed that our algebra corresponds to some deep rooted organizational principle in human brains everywhere.

This sounds plausible in theory but there are two practical difficulties which turn out to be of major importance. The first is that, in the final stage of this process, it is easy to make it appear that the theory and the evidence fit together, but the contrary is difficult to demonstrate. Logical Positivists can therefore argue that Lévi-Strauss' theories are more or less meaningless because, in the last analysis, they cannot be rigorously tested.

The second difficulty is to understand just what is meant by the total system, 'the general object of analysis' (see p. 35), the ultimate algebraic structure of which particular cultural products are merely partial manifestations. Where is this structure located? This is a question which may be asked about all cultural systems. Where is 'a spoken language' – in de Saussure's sense (p. 57) – located? The language as a whole is external to any particular individual; in Durkheim's terminology, it is part of the collective consciousness (*conscience collective*) of all those who speak it.

But Lévi-Strauss is not much concerned with the collective consciousness of any particular social system; his quest rather is to discover the collective *unconscious* of 'the human mind' (*l'esprit humain*), and this should apply not merely to speakers of one language, but to speakers of all languages.

His endeavour sometimes leads him to make statements which suggest that the mind has an autonomy of its own which operates independently of any human individual. For example:

> *Nous ne prétendons donc pas montrer comment les hommes pensent dans les mythes mais comment les mythes se pensent dans les hommes, et à leur insu* (C.C.: 20).

There are two published English versions of this passage:

1) 'We are not, therefore claiming to show how men think the myths, but rather how the myths think themselves out in men and without men's knowledge.' (Y.F.S.: 56)

2) 'I therefore claim to show, not how men think in myths but how myths operate in men's minds without their being aware of the fact.' (R.C.: 12)

The French is ambiguous. '*Comment les mythes se pensent dans les hommes*' might be translated 'how myths are thought in men', which would reduce the degree of autonomy implied. The issue of autonomy is important.

Lévi-Strauss appears to regard cross-cultural variations of cultural phenomena – especially myth – as self-generated topological distortions of a common structure. As illustration, he refers to D'Arcy Thompson's discussion of the shapes of fish (H.N.: 606; N.M.: 676–8)[14]. The presumed autonomy implies that Lévi-Strauss can ignore the cultural context of particular variants; the mechanism which generates the observed differences is not that of adaptive evolution or functional relevance, but simply mathematical permutation. The nature of 'the human mind', which functions as a kind of randomizing computer to generate these permutations 'without being aware of the fact', is left obscure. The heresy of Lévi-Strauss' Anglo-Saxon critics – the 'empiricists' of footnote 12 – is that they start off by assuming that any local variation of a structured form, whether in biology or in culture, is functionally adapted to the local environment, so that we can only claim to understand the local peculiarities after we have taken into account the local environmental circumstances. For such critics, playing noughts and crosses with topological diagrams is not enough.[15]

However, Lévi-Strauss firmly repudiates the suggestion that he is an idealist, so we have to assume that the somewhat mysterious operations of 'the human mind' which he postulates are processes which take place in the ordinary substance of the brain. So the implications of his argument seem to be something like this:

In the course of human evolution man has developed the unique capacity to communicate by means of language and signs and not just by means of signals and triggered responses. In order that he should be able to do this it is necessary that the mechanisms of the human brain (which we do not yet understand) should embody certain capacities for making +/- distinctions, for treating the binary pairs thus formed as related couples, and for manipulating these 'relations' as in a matrix algebra. We *know* that the human brain can do this in the case of sound patterns, for structural linguistics has shown that this is one (but only one) essential element in the formation of meaningful speech: we can therefore postulate that the human brain operates in much the same way when it uses non-verbal elements of culture to form a 'sign language' and that the ultimate relational system, the algebra itself, is an attribute of human brains everywhere. But – and this is where the metaphors and the metonymy come in – we also know, not only from the way we can decode speech but more particularly from the way we apprehend music, that the human brain is capable of listening to both harmony and melody at the same time. Now the associations of sounds in harmony – an orchestral score read vertically up and down the page – is metaphoric. In terms of the diagram at p. 59 the notes belong to the system of sounds which can be made by all the assembled orchestral instruments. But the sequence of sounds in a melody – an orchestral score read horizontally across the page – is metonymic. In terms of the diagram, the notes form a syntagmatic chain derived in sequence from one instrument at a time. So it is Lévi-Strauss' bold proposition that the algebra of the brain can be represented as a rectangular matrix of at least two (but perhaps several) dimensions which can be 'read' up and down or side to side like the words of a cross-word puzzle. His thesis is that we demonstrably do this with sounds (in the way we listen to words and music) therefore it is intrinsically probable that we also do the same kind of thing when we convey messages by manipulating cultural categories other than sounds.

This is an extreme reductionist argument but on the face

of it it should help to explain not only how cultural symbols convey messages within a particular cultural milieu but how they convey messages at all. The structure of relations which can be discovered by analysing materials drawn from any one culture is an algebraic transformation of other possible structures belonging to a common set and this common set constitutes a pattern which reflects an attribute of the mechanism of all human brains. It is a grand conception; whether it is a useful one may be a matter of opinion.

4   The Structure of Myth

Lévi-Strauss on Myth has much the same fascination as
Freud on the Interpretation of Dreams, and the same kind
of weaknesses too. A first encounter with Freud is usually
persuasive; it is all so neat, it simply must be right. But
then you begin to wonder. Supposing the whole Freudian
argument about symbolic associations and layers of conscious, unconscious and pre-conscious were entirely false,
would it ever be possible to *prove* that it is false? And if the
answer to that question is 'No', you then have to ask yourself
whether psycho-analytic arguments about symbol formation and free association can ever be anything better than
clever talk.

Lévi-Strauss' discussions about the structure of myth are
certainly very clever talk; whether they are really any more
than that still remains to be seen.

Myth is an ill defined category. Some people use the word
as if it meant fallacious history – a story about the past
which we know to be false; to say that an event is 'mythical'
is equivalent to saying that it didn't happen. The theological
usage is rather different: myth is a formulation of religious
mystery – 'the expression of unobservable realities in terms
of observable phenomena' (Schniewind (1953): 47). This
comes close to the anthropologist's usual view that 'myth
is a sacred tale'.

If we accept this latter kind of definition the special quality of myth is not that it is false but that it is divinely true

for those who believe, but fairy-tale for those who do not. The distinction that history is true and myth is false is quite arbitrary. Nearly all human societies posses a corpus of tradition about their own past. It starts, as the Bible starts, with a story of the Creation. This is necessarily 'mythical' in *all* senses of the term. But the Creation stories are followed by legends about the exploits of culture heroes (e.g. King David and King Solomon), which *might* have *some* foundation in 'true history', and these in turn lead on to accounts of events which everyone accepts as 'fully historical' because their occurrence has been independently recorded in some other source. The Christian New Testament purports to be history from one point of view and myth from another, and he is a rash man who seeks to draw a sharp line between the two.

Lévi-Strauss has evaded this issue of the relation between myth and history by concentrating his attention on 'societies with no history', that is to say on peoples like the Australian Aborigines and the tribal peoples of Brazil who think of their own society as changeless, and conceive of time present as a straightforward perpetuation of time past. In Lévi-Strauss' usage, myth has no location in chronological time, but it does have certain characteristics which it shares with dreams and fairy-tales. In particular, the distinction between Nature and Culture which dominates normal human experience largely disappears. In Lévi-Straussian myth men converse with animals or marry animal spouses, they live in the sea or in the sky, they perform feats of magic as a matter of course.

Here as elsewhere Lévi-Strauss' ultimate concern is with 'the unconscious nature of collective phenomena' (S.A.: 18). Like Freud he seeks to discover principles of thought formation which are universally valid for all human minds. These universal principles (if they exist) are operative in our brains just as much as in the brains of South American Indians, but in our case the cultural training we have received through living in a high technology society and through attending school or university has overlaid the universal logic of primitive thought with all kinds of special logics required by the artificial conditions of our social environment. If we are to get at the primitive universal logic, in its uncontaminated form, we need to examine the thought processes of very primitive, technologically unsophisticated, peoples (like the South American Indians), and the study of myth is one way of achieving this end.

Even if we accept the general proposition that there must be a kind of universal inbuilt logic of a non-rational kind which is shared by all humanity and which is made manifest in primitive mythology, we are still faced with many methodological difficulties. Mythology (in Lévi-Strauss' sense) starts out as an oral tradition associated with religious ritual. The tales themselves are usually transmitted in exotic languages at enormous length. By the time they become available to Lévi-Strauss, or to any other would-be analyst, they have been written down and transcribed, in abbreviated form, into one or other of the common European languages. In the process they have become completely divorced from their original religious context. This is just as true of the stories which Lévi-Strauss discusses in *Mythologiques* as it is of the myths of Greece and Rome and Ancient Scandinavia with which we are more familiar. Even so, Lévi-Strauss asserts that the stories will have retained the essential *structural* characteristics which they possessed in the first place, so that if we go about it in the right way a comparison of these emasculated stories can still be made to exhibit the outstanding characteristics of a universal primitive non-rational logic.

Our valuation of such an improbable credo can only be assessed in operational terms. If, by applying Lévi-Strauss' techniques of analysis to an actual body of anthropological materials, we are able to arrive at insights which we did not have before, and these insights throw illumination on other related ethnographic facts, which we had not considered in the first instance, then we may feel that the exercise has been worth while. And let me say at once that, in many cases, there *is* a pay-off of this kind.

The problem, as Lévi-Strauss sees it, is roughly this. If we consider any corpus of mythological tales at their face value we get the impression of an enormous variety of trivial incident, associated with a great deal of repetition, and a recurrent harping on very elementary themes: incest between brother and sister or mother and son, patricide and fratricide, cannibalism ... Lévi-Strauss postulates that behind the manifest sense of the stories there must be another non-sense (cf. p. 42 above), a message wrapped up in code. In other words he assumes with Freud that a myth is a kind of collective dream and that it should be capable of interpretation so as to reveal the hidden meaning.

Lévi-Strauss' ideas about the nature of the code and the kind of interpretation that might be possible have several sources.

The first of these comes from Freud; myths express unconscious wishes which are somehow inconsistent with conscious experience. Among primitive peoples the continuity of the political system is dependent upon the perpetuation of alliances between small groups of kin. These alliances are created and cemented by gifts of women: fathers give away their daughters, brothers give away their sisters. But if men are to give away their women to serve social-political ends they must refrain from keeping these women to themselves for sexual ends. Incest and exogamy are therefore opposite sides of the same penny and the incest taboo (a rule about sexual behaviour) is the corner stone of society (a structure of social and political relations). (See also Chapter 6.) This moral principle implies that, in the imaginary situation, 'the First Man' should have had a wife who was not his sister. But in that case any story about a 'First Man' or a 'First Woman' must contain a logical contradiction. For if they were brother and sister then we are all the outcome of pri-maeval incest, but, if they were separate creations, only one of them can be the first human being and the other must be (in some sense) other than human: thus the Biblical Eve is of one flesh with Adam and their relations are incestuous, but the non-Biblical Lilith was a demon![16]

Another 'contradiction' of a comparable kind is that the concept of life entails the concept of death; a living thing is that which is not dead, a dead thing is that which is not alive. But religion endeavours to separate these two intrinsically interdependent concepts so that we have myths which account for the *origin* of death or which represent death as 'the gateway to eternal life'. Lévi-Strauss has argued that when we are considering the universalist aspects of primitive mythology we shall repeatedly discover that the hidden message is concerned with the resolution of unwelcome contradictions of this sort. The repetitions and prevarications of mythology so fog the issue that irresolvable logical inconsistencies are lost sight of even when they are openly expressed. In 'The Story of Asdiwal' (1960), which is for many people, the most satisfying of all Lévi-Strauss' essays in myth analysis his conclusion is that:

'All the paradoxes conceived by the native mind, on the most diverse planes: geographic, economic, sociological, and even cosmological, are, when all is said and done, assimilated to that less obvious yet so real paradox which marriage with the matrilateral cousin attempts but fails to resolve. But the failure is *admitted* in our myths, and there precisely lies their function' (G.A.: 27–8).

But the 'admission' is of a complex kind and even Lévi-Strauss needs two pages of close argument to persuade the reader (who is already in possession of all the relevant evidence) that this is what in fact the myths are saying.

The second major source of Lévi-Strauss' thinking on this topic comes from arguments taken over from the field of general information theory. Myth is not just fairy-tale, it contains a message. Admittedly it is not very clear who is sending the message, but it is clear who is receiving it. The novices of the society who hear the myths for the first time are being indoctrinated by the bearers of tradition – a tradition, which in theory at any rate, has been handed down from long dead ancestors. Let us then think of the Ancestors (A) as 'senders' and the present generation (B) as 'receivers'.

Now let us imagine the situation of an individual A who is trying to get a message to a friend B who is almost out of earshot and let us suppose that communication is further hampered by various kinds of interference – noise from wind, passing cars and so on. What will A do? If he is sensible he will not be satisfied with shouting his message just once, he will shout it several times, and give a different wording to the message each time, supplementing his words with visual signals. At the receiving end B may very likely get the meaning of each of the individual messages slightly wrong, but when he puts them together the redundancies and the mutual consistencies and inconsistencies will make it quite clear what is 'really' being said.

Suppose for example that the intended message consists of 8 elements, and that each time that A shouts across to B different parts of the message get obliterated by interference from other noises then the total pattern of what B receives will consist of a series of 'chords' as in an orchestra score thus:

```
I  2     4          7  8
   2  3  4     6        8
I        4  5        7  8
I  2        5     7
      3  4  5  6        8
```

Lévi-Strauss' postulate is that a corpus of mythology constitutes an 'orchestra score' of this sort. The collectivity of the senior members of the society, through its religious institutions, is unconsciously transmitting to the junior members a basic message which is manifest in the 'score' as a whole rather than in any particular myth.

Many social anthropologists of the more usual Anglo-American sort – the functionalists of whom Lévi-Strauss is so critical – are prepared to go along with him so far, but they find his method far less acceptable when he ignores the cultural limitations of time and space.

In 'The Story of Asdiwal' which I have mentioned already Lévi-Strauss devotes 40 pages to the analysis of a single complex of myths precisely located in a particular cultural region and the result is entirely fascinating. But when, like Frazer, he roams about the ethnographies of the whole world picking up odd details of custom and story to reveal what he presumes to be a single unitary message inherent in the architecture of the human mind, most of his British admirers get left behind. Here is an example of this latter procedure:

'As in archaic China and certain Amerindian societies there was until recently a European custom which entailed the ritual extinction and subsequent rekindling of domestic hearths preceded by fasting and by the use of instruments of darkness (*instruments des tenèbres*)' (M.C.: 351).

The concept of 'instruments of darkness' refers to a 12th Century European custom in which, between Good Friday and Easter Eve, the ordinary Church bells were silent and were replaced by various other noise-producing devices the din from which was supposed to remind the faithful of the prodigies and terrifying sounds which accompanied the death of Christ (M.C.: 348). In the cited quotation Lévi-Strauss has given this mediaeval European Christian category a world wide extension by using it to include any kind of musical instrument which is employed as a signal to mark the beginning or end of a ritual performance. He then draws attention to the use of such signals in various situations where lights and fires are extinguished and rekindled at the beginning and end of a period of fast. And finally he comes back to Europe and notes that 'instruments of darkness' are used in contexts of the latter kind. The whole argument is circular since the universality of the conjunction of 'instruments of darkness' and fasting is already presupposed in the operational definition of the terms employed.

Very substantial sections of all four published volumes of *Mythologiques* are open to objections of this kind and, to be frank, this grand survey of the mythology of the Americas, which extends to 2000 pages and gives details of 813 different stories and their variants, often degenerates into a latter day *Golden Bough* with all the methodological defects which such a comment might imply. Lévi-Strauss is of course well aware that he is open to criticism of this kind and in *Mythologiques* III (O.M.: 11–12; O.T.M.: 17–18) he goes to some lengths to justify an astonishing claim that a Tukuna myth which is 'impossible to interpret' in its native South American context becomes comprehensible when brought into association with a 'paradigmatic system' drawn from the myths of North America. It seems to me that only the most uncritical devotees are likely to be persuaded by this argument.[17] But, even so, the Structural Analysis of Myth deserves our serious attention. Just what does this expression mean?

I shall try to explain by demonstration but I must emphasize two preliminary points. Firstly, a full exposition of the method requires a great deal of space; my skeletal examples give no indication of the subleties of the technique. Secondly, Lévi-Strauss' method is not entirely new. In England, Hocart and Lord Raglan made gropings in the same direction over forty years ago, so did the Russian folklorist Vladimir Propp (see V.P., 1960). Rather later, George Dumezil, one of Lévi-Strauss' senior colleagues at the Collège de France, began to develop ideas which run parallel to those of Lévi-Strauss in quite a number of ways, but the latter has carried the theoretical analysis of what he is up to much further than any of the others.

In Lévi-Strauss' first essay on this topic (S.S.M., 1955) he uses, as one of his examples, a very abbreviated analysis of the structure of the Oedipus story. This is one of the very few cases in which he has so far applied his method to a myth which is likely to be generally familiar to an English or American reader so let us start with that. In what follows I have followed Lévi-Strauss fairly closely, only introducing modifications at points where his argument seems particularly obscure.

He first assumes that the myth (any myth) can readily be

broken up into segments or incidents, and that everyone familiar with the story will agree as to what these incidents are. The incidents in every case refer to the 'relations' between the individual characters in the story, or to the 'status' of particular individuals. It is these 'relations' and 'statuses' which are the points on which we need to focus our attention; the individual characters, as such, are often interchangeable.

In the particular case of the Oidipus myth[18] he takes the following segments of a syntagmatic chain:

   i. 'Kadmos seeks his sister Europe, ravished by Zeus'
   ii. 'Kadmos kills the Dragon'
   iii. 'The Spartoi (the men who are born as a result of sowing the Dragon's teeth) kill one another'
   iv. 'Oidipus kills his father Laios'
   v. 'Oidipus kills the Sphinx' (But in fact, in the story, the Sphinx commits suicide after Oidipus has answered the riddle)
   vi. 'Oidipus marries his mother Jokaste'
   vii. 'Eteokles kills his brother Polyneikes'
   viii. 'Antigone buries her brother Polyneikes despite prohibition'

Lévi-Strauss also draws our attention to a peculiarity of three of the names:

ix.	Labdakos	— father of Laios —	= 'Lame'
x.	Laios	— father of Oidipus —	= 'Left-sided'
xi.	Oidipus		= 'Swollen foot'

Lévi-Strauss admits that the selection of these characters and these incidents is to some extent arbitrary, but he argues that if we added more incidents they would only be variations of the ones we have already. This is true enough. For example: Oidipus' task is to kill the Sphinx; he does this by answering the riddle: the answer to the riddle, according to some authorities, was – 'the child grows into an adult who grows into an old man'; the Sphinx then commits suicide; Oidipus ('the child grown into an adult') then marries his mother Jokaste; when Oidipus learns the answer to *this* riddle, Jokaste commits suicide and Oidipus puts out his own eyes to become an old man. So also, if we were to pursue the fortunes of Antigone, we should note that, having 'buried' her dead brother in defiance of the command of her mother's brother (Kreon), she is in turn herself buried alive by Kreon; she commits suicide; her suicide is followed by that of her betrothed cousin Haimon and also that of Haimon's mother Eurydike.

But where should we stop? In another version Haimon is killed by the Sphinx; in another Antigone bears Haimon a son who is killed by Kreon and so on . . .

So let us stick to Lévi-Strauss' own skeletal version. He puts his eleven segments into four columns, thus:

I	II	III	IV
(i) Kadmos-Europe			
	(iii) Spartoi	(ii) Kadmos-Dragon	
	(iv) Oidipus-Laios		(ix) Lame Labdakos
		(v) Oidipus-Sphinx	(x) Left-sided Laios
(vi)Oidipus-Jokaste			
	(vii) Eteokles-Polyneikes		(xi) Swollen-footed Oidipus
(viii) Antigone-Polyneikes			

He then points out that in each of the incidents in Column I there is a ritual offence of the nature of incest – 'an overvaluation of kinship'. This contrasts with the incidents in Column II where the offences are of the nature of fratricide/ patricide – 'an undervaluation of kinship'. In Column III the common element is the destruction of anomalous monsters by men, whereas Column IV refers to men who are themselves to some extent anomalous monsters. Here Lévi-Strauss introjects a general proposition based on grand scale comparative ethnography of the Frazerian kind:

> 'In mythology it is a universal characteristic of men born from the Earth that at the moment they emerge from the depth they either cannot walk or they walk clumsily. This is the case of the chthonian beings in the mythology of the Pueblo ... [and of] the Kwakiutl ...'

This, so he says, explains the peculiarity of the names (ix, x, xi).

Anyway, the nature of the anomalous monsters in Column III is that they are half man – half animal and the story of the sowing of the dragon's teeth implies a doctrine of the autochthonous origin of man – the Spartoi were born from the earth without human aid. In contrast, the story of Oidipus being exposed at birth and staked to the ground (this was the origin of his swollen foot) implies that even though born of woman he was not fully separated from his natural earth.

And so, says Lévi-Strauss, Column III, in which the monsters are overcome, signifies *denial of the autochthonous origin of man*, while Column IV signifies the *persistence of the autochthonous origin of man*. So IV is the converse of III just as II is the converse of I!!

By this hair-splitting logic we end up with an equation:

I/II :: III/IV

But Lévi-Strauss maintains that there is more to this than algebra. The formal religious theory of the Greeks was that man was autochthonous. The first man was half a serpent, he grew from the earth as plants grow from the earth. Therefore the puzzle that needs to be solved is:

> 'how to find a satisfactory transition between this theory and the knowledge that human beings are actually born from the union of man and woman. Although the problem obviously cannot be solved, the Oidipus myth provides a kind of logical tool which relates the original problem – born from one or born from two – to the derivative problem: born from different or born from the same. By a correlation of this type, 'the overrating of blood relations' is to 'the underrating of blood relations' as 'the attempt to escape autochthony' is to 'the impossibility to succeed in it'. Although experience contradicts theory, social life validates cosmology by its similarity of structure. Hence cosmology is true' (S.A.: 216).[19]

Those who think that all this is vaguely reminiscent of an argument from *Alice Through the Looking Glass* will not be far wrong. Lewis Carroll, in his *alter ego* as mathematician, was one of the originators of the peculiar kind of binary logic upon which Lévi-Straussian discourse and modern computer technology are alike constructed!

It must be admitted that, emasculated in this way, the argument almost ceases to be comprehensible, yet even so, as at p. 42, the reader may suspect that behind the non-sense there is a sense. The reason why Lévi-Strauss has not pursued his explorations of Classical Greek mythology any further seems to be that, in the somewhat bowdlerized form in which these stories have come down to us, there are too few parameters. The South American mythology, which has provided the main arena of his explorations, has many more dimensions. In particular he is there able to show that:

1. sets of relationships among human beings in terms of relative status, friendship and hostility, sexual availability, mutual dependence

may be represented in myth, either in direct or transposed form, as

2. relationships between different kinds (species) of men, animals, birds, reptiles, insects, supernatural beings

3. relationships between categories of food and modes of food preparation and the use or non-use of fire (see p. 41)

4. relations between categories of sound and silence produced either naturally as animal cries or artificially by means of musical instruments

5. relations between categories of smell and taste – pleasant/unpleasant, sweet/sour etc.

6. relations between types of human dress and undress and between the animals and plants from which the clothing is derived

7. relations between body functions: e.g. eating, excretion, urination, vomiting, copulation, birth, menstruation

8. relations between categories of landscape, seasonal change, climate, time alternations, celestial bodies . . .

or combinations of any of these frames of reference. The main purpose of his South American analysis is not merely to show that such symbolization occurs, for Freud and his followers have already claimed to demonstrate this, but to show that the transformations follow strictly logical rules.

Lévi-Strauss displays quite extraordinary ingenuity in the way he exhibits this hidden logic but the argument is extremely complicated and very difficult to evaluate.

Is it possible to present a reduced model of such a system of analysis and still convey the general sense?

In his original article Lévi-Strauss remarks at the end of his brief discussion of Oidipus that:

> 'If a myth is made up of all its variants, structural analysis should take them all into account. After analysing all the known variants of the Theban version, we should thus treat the others in the same way: first the tales about Labdakos' collateral line including Agave, Pentheus, and Jokaste herself; the Theban version about Lykos with Amphion and Zetos as the city founders; more remote variants concerning Dionysos (Oidipus' matrilateral cousin) and Athenian legends where Kekrops takes the place of Kadmos. For each of them a similar chart should be drawn and then compared and reorganized according to the findings . . .' (S.A.: 217).

The methodological programme applied to American materials in *Mythologiques* is a modification of this plan. Vol. I starts with a Bororo myth from South America (M.1) and explores variants and permutations. There is recurrent emphasis on the theme that: 'culinary operations are viewed as mediatory activities between heaven and earth, life and death, nature and society' (R.C.: 64–65). Vol. II examines more convoluted versions of the same complex and Vol. III pursues the chase into North America. Vol. IV leads us the other way round. Starting with a myth from the American North West (M.529),[20] variants eventually take us back to South America. The emphasis on cooking as an agent of transformation persists, but the title *Naked Man* draws attention to the recurrent equivalence: naked/clothed = Nature/Culture. At the end of the day Lévi-Strauss claims to have demonstrated that the whole vast agglomeration of stories forms a single system. In principle, such an operation might be expanded indefinitely so there can be nothing heretical about applying the rules of the game to the mythology of Classical Greece. There are indeed striking American parallels for some well known European themes (Hultkrantz, 1957).

In particular Orpheus, being heavily laden with binary antithesis, seems positively to invite a Lévi-Straussian investigation:

> He is a son of gentle Apollo but a follower of wild Dionysos, with whom he becomes identified.

> He rescues his wife from the land of the dead by means of music but loses her because of silence – 'not hearing her footsteps behind him'

> He is a devoted husband yet the originator of male homosexuality; his oracle was located on Lesbos the traditional source of female homosexuality . . .

Furthermore the Orpheus–Euridike story is a structural permutation of the Demeter-Persephone story:

> Euridike the wife and Persephone the Virgin Daughter are both carried off to rule as Queen of the Underworld. Orpheus the husband fails to rescue his wife and is sterile;

Demeter the mother partially rescues her daughter and is fertile.

Euridike dies in consequence of being bitten by a snake while evading the sexual embraces of Aristaios, half-brother to Orpheus. The punishment of Aristaios is that he loses his bees and hence his honey.

He recovers his bees by finding a swarm in the carcass of a sacrificed animal which has been specially allowed to go *putrid* instead of being *cooked and burned* for the gods in the usual way.

Persephone fails to achieve immortality because she eats *raw* pomegranate seeds in the other world; her foster brother Demophoon nearly achieves immortality because he eats nothing in this world but is instead anointed with ambrosia, a food of the gods related to honey. He fails to achieve immortality because his real mother (Metaneira) drags him from fire in which he is being *cooked* by Demeter, who is seeking to burn away his mortality. Persephone is lured to her doom by the fragrant smell of fresh flowers . . .

Already I have started enough hares to fill a whole volume of Lévi-Strauss' *magnum opus* and our author himself is undoubtedly aware of the possibilities (see e.g. M.C., 347a). But the ordinary reader who is unfamiliar with the details of Classical mythology or of the permutations and combinations of *Mythologiques* can hardly be expected to decipher such a rigmarole. So I shall attempt something much more modest. By following through a very restricted version of Lévi-Strauss' original plan (p. 81), I shall try to give the reader some feeling of how, in a Structuralist analysis, the contrasted patterns of superficially different stories can be seen to fit together. It needs to be realized, however, that in any such truncated illustration we necessarily forfeit many of the subtler nuances of the technique.

Within these limitations the analysis which follows, which discusses eight stories in outline and mentions several others in skeletal form, is intended to illustrate certain of the key features in Lévi-Strauss' procedure. The various stories are all summarized in the same way so that the roles of the various *dramatis personae* can be easily distinguished. King, Queen, Mother, Father, Brother, Sister, Daughter, Son-in-law, Paramour etc. are seen to exhibit permutations of a single 'plot'.

The comparison rests on a basic underlying hypothesis to the effect that Greek mythology as a whole constitutes a single 'system' (language) and that each individual story is a syntagm of that 'system' (see p. 58). The system as a whole presupposes a certain metaphorical apprehension of the relative positions of men and animals and deities in a matrix formed by the oppositions:

ABOVE/BELOW, THIS WORLD/OTHER WORLD,
CULTURE/NATURE

This schema is summarized in the diagram displayed in Fig. 5. Other factors which are presupposed in my analysis (but this would be more evident if my description of the myths were more complete) are the transformational rules which have been hinted at in my remarks about the Orpheus story on p. 82. The Greek deities were supposed to eat only fresh uncooked foods – ambrosia, nectar, (?) honey – but they delighted in the *smell* of burnt offerings, thus BURNING/PUTRID :: SKY/UNDERWORLD. In my versions of the myths the issue is blatantly about sex and homicide; in a fuller account it would be seen that this issue also appears in other guises transposed onto other planes. Just *how* this works cannot be shown in brief space but the following generalization by Lévi-Strauss derived from his American material may well apply to the Greek data also:

'[there is] an analogy between honey and menstrual blood. Both are transformed (*élaborée*) substances resulting from a sort of *infra-cuisine*, vegetal in the one case ... animal in the other. Moreover honey may be either healthy or toxic, just as a woman in her normal condition is "a honey", but secretes a poison when she is indisposed. Finally we have seen that, in native thought, the search for honey represents a sort of return to Nature, in the guise of erotic attraction transposed from the sexual register to that of the sense of taste, which undermines the very foundations of Culture if it is indulged in for too long. In the same way the *honey*-moon will be a menace to public order if the bridal pair are allowed to extend their private game indefinitely and to neglect their duties to society' (O.M.: 340; O.T.M.: 412–13).

And if the relevance of all this to what follows seems obscure I can only remark that one of the unmentioned characters, Glaukos, son of Minos and brother-in-law to Dionysos was 'drowned in a jar of honey' and reborn from a tomb!

Finally I should point out that the ultimate conclusion of the analysis is not that 'all the myths say the same thing' but that 'collectively the sum of what all the myths say is not expressly said by any of them, and that what they thus say (collectively) is a necessary poetic truth which is an unwelcome contradiction'. It is Lévi-Strauss' thesis that the function of mythology is to exhibit publicly, though in disguise, ordinarily unconscious paradoxes of this kind (cf. p. 72).

PRESUMED SCHEMA

FIG. 5

The underlying assumption throughout the analysis is that the 'reduced model' of Fig. 5 which arranges various pairs of categories in binary opposition along two axes up and down and left and right is implicit in the whole system of mythology of which the listed stories are particular examples.

The Stories

1. *Kadmos, Europe and the Dragon's Teeth*

STORY: Zeus (God) in the form of a tame wild bull (mediator between wild and tame) seduces and carries off a human girl, Europe.

The brother, Kadmos, and the mother, Telephassa, of Europe search for her. The mother dies and is buried by Kadmos. Kadmos is then told to follow a particular cow

86

(domestic animal: replacement of the sister and the mother).
Where the cow stops, Kadmos must found Thebes, having
first sacrificed the cow to Athena. (Cow forms link
between man and gods just as bull formed link between
gods and man.) In seeking to provide water for the sacrifice
Kadmos encounters a dragon (monster) guarding a sacred
pool. The dragon is a son of Ares, God of War. Kadmos and
the dragon engage in battle. Having killed the dragon,
Kadmos sows the dragon's teeth (a domestic action applied
to wild material). The crop is men (the Spartoi) without
mothers. They kill one another, but the survivors cooperate
with Kadmos to found Thebes. Kadmos makes peace with
Ares and marries his daughter Harmonia. The gods give
Harmonia a magical necklace as dowry, which later brings
disaster to everyone who possesses it. At the end of the story
Kadmos and Harmonia change into dragons.

COMMENT: The story specifies the polarity Nature : Culture : : Gods : Men and affirms that the relationship between
Gods and Men is one of ambiguous and unstable alliance –
exemplified by marriage followed by feud followed by marriage accompanied by poisoned marriage gifts. There is also
the ambiguity of autochthony – non-autochthony. Kadmos
who slays the Dragon from whom are born the Spartoi is
himself the Dragon and ancestor of the Spartoi.

2. Minos and the Minotaur

STORY: Minos is son of Zeus and Europe (previous story)
and husband to Pasiphaë, daughter of the Sun.
Poseidon is brother to Zeus but his counterpart, god of the
sea instead of god of the sky.
Poseidon sends Minos a beautiful bull which should be

sacrificed: Minos retains the bull. In punishment Poseidon causes Pasiphaë to lust after the bull. By the ingenuity of Daidalos, Pasiphaë is changed into a cow and has sex relations with the bull, of which union is born the monster Minotaur, who annually devours a tribute of living youths and maidens.

COMMENT: This is the inverse of the first story, thus:
a. KADMOS VERSION: Bull (= Zeus) carries away Europe, who has a human child, Minos. Europe has a human brother, Kadmos, who is required to sacrifice a cow, sent from the gods, and in the process he kills a monster from whose remains come live human beings. But Kadmos is himself the monster.
b. MINOS VERSION: Bull (= Poseidon) cohabits with Pasiphaë, who has a monster child, Minotaur. Pasiphaë has a human husband, Minos, who is required to sacrifice a bull, sent from the gods (which he fails to do). The bull is replaced by a monster who consumes human beings. But the monster = Minotaur = Minos–Bull is himself Minos.

In effect, the two stories have almost identical 'structures'; one story is converted into the other by 'changing the signs', i.e. bulls become cows, brothers become husbands, and so on.

The implication is the same as before. Again we have a polarity Gods : Men :: Wild : Tame :: Monsters : Domestic Animals with the Divine Bull an ambiguous creature linking the two sides. Again sexual relations between gods and men and the sacrifice of divine animals expresses the highly equivocal alliance in which the friendship of the gods is bought only at enormous cost.

3. *Theseus, Ariadne and the Minotaur*

STORY: (skeleton). Theseus, son of Poseidon by a human mother, is ranged against Minos, son of Zeus by a human mother. Ariadne daughter of Minos and Pasiphaë (story 2) loves Theseus and betrays her father by means of a *thread*. Theseus kills the Minotaur and elopes with Ariadne but deserts her.

COMMENT: This is one of a group of closely related stories in which a father or the father's double (here Minos–Minotaur) is killed by his enemy because of the treachery of the daughter who loves the enemy; but the victorious enemy then punishes the daughter by desertion or murder. Thus:

3a. Minos is at war with Nisos, king of Megara, a descendant of the autochthonous Kekrops. Nisos is preserved from death by a magic lock of *hair*. Skylla daughter of Nisos, cuts off the hair and presents it as a love token to Minos. Minos kills Nisos but abandons Skylla in disgust. Nisos is then turned into a sea-eagle in perpetual pursuit of his errant daughter in the form of another sea bird (*keiris*).

3b. Perseus, son of Zeus by the human Danaë, is founder king of Mycenae. The kingdom passes to Perseus' son Alkaios and then to Elektryon, brother of Alkaios, who engages in feud with Pterelaos, grandson of Nestor, another brother of Alkaios. Amphitryon, son of Alkaios, is betrothed to Alkmene, daughter of Elektryon (his father's brother). Elektryon gives Amphitryon the kingdom but binds him by oath not to sleep with Alkmene until vengeance against Pterelaos has been achieved.

In the course of the feud the sons of Pterelaos drive off

Elektryon's *cows* and are counter-attacked by the sons of
Elektryon. One son from each side survives. Amphitryon
redeems the cattle but, as he is driving them home, one of
the cows runs aside. Amphitryon flings a stick at the cow
but the stick hits Elektryon who is killed. Pterelaos is,
like Nisos, preserved from death by a magic *hair*.
Komaitho, daughter of Pterelaos, in love with Amphitryon,
betrays her father (as in (3a)). Amphitryon kills Pterelaos
but also kills Komaitho for her treachery.

Notice first that the killing of Elektryon on account of an
errant *cow* is metaphoric of the killing of the other fathers
on account of an errant *daughter*. Secondly that in each case
there is a clash of loyalties, since the daughter must betray
the father in seeking to gain a husband. In the first two cases
(Theseus, Minos) the potential husband rejects the sinful
daughter but in the third case the 'contradiction' is resolved
by a duplication of roles. Pterelaos is the double of Elektryon, Komaitho is the double of Alkmene. Amphitryon kills
both the fathers but his killing of Komaitho allows him to
marry Alkmene.

3c. Alkmene now becomes the prototype of the faithful
wife. Nevertheless she is faithless since she becomes the
mother of Herakles as the result of sexual union with Zeus
who had impersonated her husband Amphitryon.

These stories add up to a variation of Lévi-Strauss' generalization as cited at p. 79. The hero who is left on stage (Theseus
in the one case, Herakles in the other) is the son of a human
mother by a divine father and therefore the opposite of the
autochthonous beings (like Kekrops) who are born of the
earth without reference to women. Yet Lévi-Strauss' formula still applies except that the 'problem' of incest ('the

overrating of blood relations') and parricide/fratricide ('the underrating of blood relations') is replaced by the 'problem' of exogamy and feud ('the overrating of affinal relations' – treachery by the errant daughter – and 'the underrating of affinal relations' – murder of the potential father-in-law by the potential son-in-law).

4. *Antiope, Zethos and Amphion*

STORY: Kadmos is succeeded as King of Thebes, first by a daughter's son Pentheus, then by his own son Polydoros, then by Labdakos son of Polydoros. Pentheus and Labdakos both become sacrifices to Dionysos – their womenfolk in a frenzy mistake them for wild beasts and tear them to pieces. Laios the next heir is an infant and the throne is usurped by Lykos the mother's father's brother of Labdakos. Antiope, daughter of Nykteus, is brother's daughter to Lykos. She becomes pregnant by Zeus. Nykteus, dishonoured, commits suicide and the duty of punishing Antiope for her liaison falls on Lykos. Lykos and his wife Dirke capture and imprison Antiope but not before she has given birth to twins, Zethos (a warrior) and Amphion (a musician) who as infants are exposed on a mountain and (like Oidipus) rescued by Shepherds. In due course the twins discover their mother and avenge themselves on Lykos and Dirke and reign jointly in Thebes.

COMMENT: This story combines features from Story 3 with those of the better-known Oidipus stories (Nos. 6 and 7 below). The role of Amphitryon in 3(b) is taken over by Zeus. The suicide of Nykteus is, in effect, a slaying of the father-in-law by the son-in-law. Zethos and Amphion are sons of Zeus by a human mother, their opponent Lykos is son of the autochthonous Chthonios. In other respects Antiope is a sort of Antigone–Jokaste. Antiope, like Antigone, is imprisoned by her uncle, but where Lykos is father's brother of Antiope, Kreon is mother's brother of Antigone. Amphion and Zethos resemble Oidipus in that they are exposed on a mountain in childhood and seize the throne after killing the King. But they kill the King after discovering their true parentage; whereas Oidipus kills the King first. They also resemble Eteokles and Polyneikes in that they are twins who both claim the throne, but they rule together in amity, one as a warrior one as a musician, whereas the Argives both being warriors, kill one another. Like Oidipus, Amphion and Zethos are 'mediators' between the sky gods and the underworld in that their mother Antiope is in the line of Chthonios and their father is Zeus. So far as the succession principle is concerned Amphion and Zethos are the opposites of the Spartoi. The Spartois are the autochthonous sons of a Chthonian man-monster – Kadmos; Amphion and Zethos are the sons of a human mother by a sky-deity Zeus. But the final outcome is disaster. Amphion marries Niobe by whom he has many children, but Niobe boasts of her fertility and the whole family is destroyed by the wrath of the gods.

MORAL: Amity between brothers (Amphion–Zethos) is ultimately no more fruitful than fratricide (Eteokles–Polyneikes) (below).

5. *Theseus, Phaidra and Hippolytos*

STORY: Hippolytos is the son of Theseus by Antiope, Queen of the Amazons. Phaidra, daughter of Minos, is wife to Theseus and step-mother to Hippolytos. Phaidra falls in love with Hippolytos who rejects her advances; Phaidra then accuses Hippolytos of having tried to rape her. In revenge Theseus appeals to Poseidon to slay Hippolytos and Hippolytos dies. Phaidra commits suicide. Theseus discovers his error and suffers remorse.

COMMENT: This is very close to being the inverse of the Oidipus story below. Here the father kills the son instead of the son killing the father. The son does not sleep with the mother, though he is accused of doing so. The mother (Phaidra–Jokaste) commits suicide in both cases; the surviving father–son (Theseus–Oidipus) suffers remorse in both cases. It will be observed that the failure of Hippolytos to commit incest with his (step-)mother Phaidra has an even • more negative outcome than the actual incest of Oidipus with Jokaste.

Notice further that Phaidra is sister to Ariadne (Story 3). The roles are now reversed. Instead of the son-in-law killing the father-in-law because of the treachery of the daughter, the father kills the son because of the treachery of the mother.

6. *Laios, Chrysippos and Jokaste*

STORY: During the reign of Lykos, Amphion and Zethos, Laios goes into banishment and is befriended by Pelops. He falls in love with Pelops' son, Chrysippos, whom he teaches to drive a chariot. After returning to the throne of Thebes he marries Jokaste but avoids sleeping with her because of the prophecy that her son will kill him. The conception which results in the birth of Oidipus follows a bout of lust when Laios has got drunk at a religious feast. On the occasion when he encounters Oidipus 'at the cross roads', Oidipus is a 'young man driving a chariot'.

COMMENT: The myth establishes an equivalence between Chrysippos and Oidipus and the incest between Oidipus and his mother is matched by homosexual incest between Laios and his son.

7. *Oidipus*

STORY: The King (Laios) and the Queen (Jokaste) rule in Thebes. The son (Oidipus) is exposed on a mountain with his ankle staked and thought to be dead. He survives. The son meets the king-father 'at a crossroads' and kills him. The Queen's brother (Kreon) acts as regent. Thebes is beset by a monster (Sphinx: female). The Queen's hand in marriage is offered to anyone who will get rid of the monster by answering its riddle. Oidipus does so. The monster commits suicide. The son assumes all aspects of the deceased father's role. On discovery, the Queen commits suicide; son-King (Oidipus) blinds himself and becomes a seer (acquires supernatural sight).

8. *Argives (Antigone, Eteokles and Polyneikes)*

STORY: Oidipus has two sons, Eteokles and Polyneikes, who are also his half-brothers since all are sons of Jokaste. Oidipus having abdicated, Eteokles and Polyneikes are supposed to hold the throne alternately. Eteokles takes the throne first and refuses to give it up; Polyneikes is banished and leads an army of heroes from Argos against Thebes. The expedition fails. Eteokles and Polyneikes kill each other. Antigone, in defiance of Kreon, performs funeral rites over Polyneikes. In punishment she is walled up alive in a tomb where she commits suicide. Later the sons of the dead heroes lead another expedition against Thebes and are triumphant.

COMMENT: Lévi-Strauss' own treatment of stories 7 and 8 in conjunction with story 1 has already been given at pp. 75–9.

It will be seen that if we proceed in this way there never comes any particular point at which we can say that we have considered 'all the variants' for almost any story drawn from the general complex of classical Greek mythology turns out to be a variant in one way or another. If, for example, we take as our central theme the Oedipus Complex as understood by Freud – the story of a son who kills his father and then becomes the paramour of his mother we shall find that the following well-known stories are all 'variants' thus:

OIDIPUS: son kills father and becomes paramour
AGAMEMNON: paramour kills father inviting vengeance from the son
ODYSSEUS: father merges with son and destroys the would-be paramours. Odysseus has no descendants.
MENELAOS: paramour (Paris) is destroyed by a third party and there is no heir (son)
HIPPOLYTOS (Story 5): innocent son falsely accused of being paramour is killed by father

What emerges from such a comparison is that each story is seen to be a combination of relational themes and that each is one of a set of variations and that what is *significant* about these relational themes is the contrast between the variations.

The 'message' contained in the whole set of stories – the ones which I have spelled out at some length and the ones

I have mentioned only by title – cannot readily be put into words, otherwise there would be no need for such circumlocution. But, roughly, what it amounts to is simple enough: If Society is to go on, daughters must be disloyal to their parents and sons must destroy (replace) their fathers.[21]

Here then is the irresolvable unwelcome contradiction, the necessary fact that we hide from consciousness because its implications run directly counter to the fundamentals of human morality. There are no heroes in these stories; they are simply epics of unavoidable human disaster. The disaster always originates in the circumstance that a human being fails to fulfil his or her proper obligations towards a deity or a kinsman and this, in part at least, is what Lévi-Strauss is getting at when he insists that the fundamental moral implication of mythology is that *'l'enfer, c'est nous-même'* which I take to mean 'self-interest is the source of all evil' (see p. 48).

But I must again remind the reader that this whole example is 'Leach imitating Lévi-Strauss' and not a summary of any Lévi-Strauss original. It has been necessary to go to this length in order to display the 'theme and variations' aspects of a typical Lévi-Straussian analysis, but in all other respects the material is thin and atypical. There is a paucity of magical happenings and a monotonous concentration on the bed-rock issues of homicide and sexual misdemeanour. In Lévi-Strauss' own examples these 'ultimate' conflicts are usually transformed into a language code of some other kind. For example, in his American case material many of the most perceptive of Lévi-Strauss' comparisons derive from analogies between eating and sexual intercourse. Close parallels are not easily found in classical mythology but the stories relating to the ancestry of Zeus, which are themselves in certain respects duplicates of the Oidipus myth, will serve as a partial illustration:

Gaea, Earth, first produces Uranos, Heaven, by spontaneous generation. Then Uranos copulates with his mother. She bears the Titans. Uranos jealous of his sons, thrusts them back into the body of their mother. Gaea unable to tolerate this state of permanent gestation arms the last of her sons Kronos with a sickle with which he castrates his father. The drops of blood fall to earth and turn into the Furies, the Giants, and the Nymphs; the castrated member itself falls to the sea and is transformed into Aphrodite the goddess of love. Kronos then rules and is in turn told that he will be overthrown by his son, but where Laios tried to save himself by abstaining from heterosexual intercourse (Story 6 above) Kronos indulges himself but swallows his children as fast as they are born. When Zeus is born, the mother, Rhea, gives Kronos a phallic shaped stone instead of the new born babe. Kronos then vomits up the stone along with all the children previously consumed.

In this story, the ordinary act of sexual intercourse is transposed. Where in 'reality' the male inserts a phallus into the female vagina and thereafter children are born through the vagina, in the myth the female inserts a phallus into the male mouth as a form of food and thereafter the children are born through the mouth in the form of vomit. A crude nursery imagery no doubt, but in Lévi-Strauss' view this exemplifies a very general principle:

'In the language (plan) of myth vomit is the correlative and inverse term of coitus and defecation is the correlative and inverse term to auditory communication' (M.C.: 210; H.A.: 246).

and by the time he has finished with it, he has linked up this symbolism with modes of cooking, methods of making fire, changes in the seasons, the menstrual periods of young women, the diet of young mothers and elderly spinsters, and Lord knows what else, but to discover just how one thing leads to another the reader must pursue some enquiries on his own. Having started at *Mythologiques* II (M.C.: 210–12; H.A.: 246–9) he will be led back to various other Lévi-Straussian references but notably to *Mythologiques* I (C.C.: 344; R.C.: 338) and 'The Structural Study of Myth' from which we started out.[22] The journey is well worth while though the traveller will not necessarily be all that the wiser when he comes to the end of it.

And let me say again that even among those who have found it extremely rewarding to apply Lévi-Strauss' Structuralist techniques to the detailed study of particular bodies of case material, there is widespread scepticism about the reckless sweep with which he himself is prepared to apply his generalizations. For example, consider the following:

With regard to the riddle of the Sphinx, Lévi-Strauss claims that it is in the nature of things that a mythical riddle should have no answer. It is also in the nature of things that a mother should not marry her own son. Oidipus contradicts nature by answering the riddle; he also contradicts nature by marrying his mother.

Now if we define a mythical riddle as 'a question which postulates that there is no answer' then the converse would be 'an answer for which there was no question'. In the Oidipus stories disaster ensues because someone answers the unanswerable question; in another class of myths of world wide distribution disaster ensues because someone fails to ask the answerable question. Lévi-Strauss cites as examples: the death of Buddha because Ananda failed to ask him to remain alive, and the disasters of the Fisher-King which are the consequence of Gawain–Percival failing to ask about the nature of the Holy Grail.

This kind of verbal juggling with a generalized formula is quite typical of Lévi-Strauss' hypothesis-forming procedure, but such methods cannot show us the truth; they only lead into a world where all things are possible and nothing sure.

5 Words and Things

Lévi-Strauss' lively but relatively brief study *La Pensée sauvage* (1962) is related to the massive but meticulously elaborated volumes of *Mythologiques* (1964, 1967, 1968, 1971) in much the same way as Freud's *The Psychopathology of Everyday Life* is related to *The Interpretation of Dreams*. In each case the shorter work endeavours to relate some of the findings of the more formal academic study to 'ordinary experience'. *La Pensée sauvage*, it is true, often strays a long way from ordinary experience; neither Totemism nor Existentialism can be rated of central concern to the average educated Englishman. All the same, there are sections of this difficult book which discuss very 'ordinary' matters such as the odd systems of naming which we apply to our pets and our garden roses! But the four year gap between the publication of the French and the English editions is an index of the problems of translation. The present English version (*The Savage Mind*) is the work of several hands. The text has the approval of Lévi-Strauss himself but has been described by an American critic as 'execrable' and the translator who was originally commissioned by the English publishers has repudiated all responsibility! Trouble starts even with the title. The obvious translation of *La Pensée sauvage* would have been 'Savage Thought', a version supported by the somewhat baffling dustjacket of the original French edition which displayed an illustration of wild pansies, purposely recalling Shakespeare's 'there is pansies, that's for thoughts'. The actual title, *The Savage Mind*, drags us back to *l'esprit humain* – the human mind – which, as we have seen, is hard to rescue from the metaphysical implications of Hegel's *Geist* or Durkheim's 'Collective Consciousness'. But in fact *La Pensée sauvage* is not really concerned with metaphysics at all, it is about logic.

The fundamental theme is that we are at fault if we follow Lévy-Bruhl (and by derivation Sartre) in thinking that there is an historical contrast between the 'pre-logical' mentality of Primitives and the 'logical' mentality of Modern Man. Primitive people are no more mystical in their approach to reality than we are. The distinction rather is between a logic which is constructed out of observed contrasts in the sensory qualities of concrete objects – e.g. the difference between raw and cooked, wet and dry, male and female – and a logic which depends upon the formal contrasts of entirely abstract entities – e.g. + and – or $\log \times$ and x^e. The latter kind of logic, which even in our own society, is used only by highly specialized experts, is a different way of talking about the same kind of thing. Primitive thought differs from scientific thought much as the use of an abacus differs from mental arithmetic, but the fact that, in our present age, we are coming to depend on things outside ourselves – such as computers – to help us with our problems of communication and calculation makes this an appropriate moment to examine the way that primitive people likewise are able to make sense of the events of daily life by reference to codes composed of things outside themselves – such as the attributes of animal species.

As an indication of just how complicated this 'logic of the concrete' is supposed to be I give below a quotation from *Mythologiques* II which ties in an argument about categories of musical instruments with an argument about categories of food, modes of food preparation and types of container. In this particular example the ethnographic evidence is all drawn from the cultural context of South American Indians but Lévi-Strauss maintains that much the same permutations and combinations will hold good everywhere. The passage quoted assumes that we are familiar with the general frame of discourse which has been developed in *Mythologiques* I and the earlier parts of *Mythologiques* II. One aspect of this may be illustrated by going back to my prime example about traffic lights (p. 31 f.) and then turning to the Table at p. 59. In the latter the 'systems' of garments, food, furniture etc. can be subjected to permutation just as are my three colours. So too with types of sound.

With light signals we can convey messages by varying the frequency and duration of the light flashes, changing the colours and so on, but the most basic distinction is simply to turn the lights on and off. So too with dress, the most radical distinction is naked/clothed, with music, it is noise/silence.

Hence it emerges that in the pages of *Mythologiques* certain basic oppositions are constantly being reiterated and combined into patterns. These include not only the paired dimensions incorporated in the Culinary Triangle (pp. 40–1) and the schema of Fig. 5 (p. 86) but also a number of others, notably light/darkness, noise/silence, naked/clothed, sacred/profane.

A newcomer is bound to feel very puzzled as to why such a seemingly random set of dichotomies should be felt to cohere together to form a single macro-set, and it is a measure of Lévi-Strauss' intellectual achievement that he is able to establish a fairly convincing case for holding that this is so. Without prejudging that larger issue I can at least illustrate part of such a total 'system' from a well known example. In classical mythology thunder (noise) expresses the anger of Zeus (sacred) whose drink is nectar, a distillation of (fresh) flowers (Nature). Incidentally it seems to be generally true that, in the language of ancient and primitive mythologies, which did not need to cope with the cacophony of our industrial age, loud noises are *always* an attribute of the divine. Readers who find this implausible should remember that even in Christian eschatology, the end of everything, which is also the day of judgement, will be announced by a trumpet call, and that until quite recent times church bells were much the loudest noise that ordinary individuals ever had to endure.

But let me get back to my promised example of the Logic of the concrete. In *Mythologiques* II the themes of honey and tobacco are seen as the 'penumbra of cooking' (*les entours de la cuisine*) and their contrasts are said to correspond, in the logic of mythology, to contrasts 'internal to the category of noise' such as the opposition: continuous sound *versus* discontinuous sound or modulated sound *versus* unmodulated sound. The argument is that objects and the sensory characteristics of things 'out there' are manipulated by the brain, through the thought system incorporated in myth, just as if they were symbols in a mathematical equation. Here is my specimen quotation:

'When used as a ritual rattle (*hochet*) the calabash is an instrument of sacred music, utilized in conjunction with tobacco which the myths conceive under the form of (an item of) culture included within nature; but when used to hold water and food, the calabash is an instrument of profane cooking, a container destined to receive natural products, and thus appropriate as an illustration of the inclusion of nature within culture. And it is the same for the hollow tree which, as a drum, is an instrument of music whose summoning role is primarily social, and which when holding honey, has to do with nature if it is a question of fresh honey being enclosed within its interior, and with culture if it is a question of honey being put to ferment within the trunk of a tree which is not hollow by nature but hollowed artificially to make it into a trough' (M.C.: 406–7; H.A.: 472–3).

If Lévi-Strauss is justified in believing that primitive people think like that then quite clearly the Frazer–Lévy-Bruhl–Sartre notion that primitive thought is characterized by naïveté, childishness, superstition and so on is wholly misplaced. Lévi-Strauss' primitives are just as sophisticated as we are, it is simply that they use a different system of notation.

But is he justified? The sceptics have no difficulty about finding points for criticism. The ethnographic worry is that Lévi-Strauss may have unconsciously selected his evidence so as to fit his theory, very much as Frazer used to do. His evidence *illustrates* his theory, but suppose he had chosen other evidence might not the whole argument fall to pieces? At this stage in the demonstration, he had already made reference to 353 different myths, but there is a great deal of other rather similar stuff which he might have used, and we have to take it on trust that it really all says the same thing. In actual fact, despite the convolutions and complexity, I think this particular case does stand up, but the fault, if there is one, is that Lévi-Strauss tries to make his mathematics of manipulated sensory objects too systematic. He fails to allow for the fact that whereas the symbols used by mathematicians are emotionally neutral – ix is not more *exciting* than x just because i is an imaginary number – the concrete symbols used in primitive thought are heavily loaded with taboo valuations. Consequently psychological factors such as evasion and repression tend to confuse the logical symmetries. This does not mean that Lévi-Strauss' calculus must be invalid, but it may be much less precise than he seems to suggest. Or to put the same point another way: Because he takes his cue from Jakobson-style linguistic theory and the mechanics of digital computers, Lévi-Strauss tends to imply – as is clearly shown in the long quotation cited above – that the whole structure of primitive thought is binary. Now there is not the slightest doubt that the human brain does have a tendency to operate with binary counters in all sorts of situations – but it can operate in other ways as well. A fully satisfactory mechanical model of the human mind would certainly contain many analog features which do *not* occur in digital computers. So far, the Lévi-Straussian scheme of analysis has not taken this into account.[23]

Even so, novices who tackle *The Savage Mind* as their introduction to the mind of Lévi-Strauss will, if they are patient, get an enormous brain twisting enjoyment out of the first eight chapters. True, they will not be in a position to judge whether Lévi-Strauss is correct in claiming that his mytho-logic is a universal human characteristic, but they will certainly begin to see some of their own familiar behaviour in a new light. I would commend in particular the extensive discussion of our conventions concerning the names which we give to animals which forms part of a chapter entitled 'The Individual as a Species'. The basic point here is that, with us, dogs, as pets, are a part of human society but not quite human and this is expressed when we give them names which are like human names but nearly always slightly different from real human names (or so

Lévi-Strauss insists). On the other hand when we give nicknames to birds – e.g. Jenny Wren, Tom Tit, Jack Daw, Robin Redbreast – they are normal human names. The difference is that the 'non-human' names of pet dogs are names of individuals, whereas the 'human' names of birds are applied indiscriminately to any member of a whole species. This is the distinction between metonymic and metamorphic modes of symbolic association which was discussed above (pp. 60–5). Lévi-Strauss' comment is as follows:

'Birds are given human christian names in accordance with the species to which they belong more easily than are other zoological classes, because they can be permitted to resemble men for the very reason that they are so different. They are feathered, winged, oviparous and they are also physically separated from human society by the element in which it is their privilege to move. As a result of this fact, they form a community which is independent of our own but, precisely because of this independence, appears to us like another society, homologous to that in which we live: birds love freedom; they build themselves homes in which they live a family life and nurture their young; they often engage in social relations with other members of their species; and they communicate with them by acoustic means recalling articulated language.'

'Consequently everything objective conspires to make us think of the bird world as a metaphorical human society: is it not after all literally parallel to it on another level? There are countless examples in mythology and folklore to indicate the frequency of this mode of representation.'

'The position is exactly the reverse in the case of dogs. Not only do they not form an independent society; as "domestic" animals they are part of human society, although with so low a place in it that we should not dream of . . . designating them in the same way as human beings . . . On the contrary, we allot them a special series: "Azor", "Medor", "Sultan", "Fido", "Diane" (the last of these is of course a human christian name but in the first instance conceived as mythological). Nearly all these are like stage names, forming a series parallel to the names people bear in ordinary life or, in other words, metaphorical names. Consequently when the relation between (human and animal) species is socially conceived as metaphorical, the relation between the respective systems of naming takes on a metonymical character; and when the relation between species is conceived as metonymical, the system of naming assumes a metaphorical character' (S.M.: 204, 205).

The catch of course, as any pet-loving Englishman will immediately recognize, is that these broad French generalizations do *not* hold up as soon as we cross the Straits of Dover! A great many English dogs have names *identical* with those of our human friends! Be that as it may, Lévi-Strauss then goes on to make further learned generalizations about the names which French farmers give to their cows:

'Now the names given to cattle belong to a different series from birds' or dogs'. They are generally descriptive terms referring to the colour of their coats, their bearing or temperament: "Rustaud", "Russet", "Blanchette", "Douce" etc. these names have a metaphorical character but they differ from the names given to dogs in that they are epithets coming from the syntagmatic chain while the latter come from the paradigmatic series; the former thus tend to derive from speech, the latter from language' (S.M.: 206).

Here again, the Englishman is out of line though we do better when it comes to racehorses! The trouble is that Lévi-Strauss always wants to force his evidence into moulds which are completely symmetrical:

'If therefore birds are *metaphorical human beings* and dogs *metonymical human beings*, cattle may be thought of as *metonymical inhuman beings* and racehorses as *metaphorical inhuman beings*. Cattle are contiguous only for want of similarity, racehorses similar only for want of contiguity. Each of these two categories offers the converse image of one of the two other categories, which themselves stand in the relation of inverted symmetry' (S.M.: 207).

But supposing the English evidence doesn't really fit? Well no matter, the English are an illogical lot of barbarians in any case.

Don't misunderstand me. *The Savage Mind* taken as a whole is an entrancing book. The exploration of the way we (the Primitives and the Civilized alike) use different kinds of language for purposes of classification, and of the way that the categories which relate to social (cultural) space are interwoven with the categories which relate to natural space is packed with immensely stimulating ideas. But you should not always believe what is said! When, for example, in the context outlined above, Lévi-Strauss claims that the names of racehorses have the quality they do have *because* racehorses

'do not form part of human society either as subjects or
objects. Rather, they constitute the desocialized condition of existence of a private society; that which lives
off race-courses or frequents them' (S.M.: 206).

The train of thought is fascinating, but what sort of 'truth'
is involved? Even if we grant that the names given to racehorses form a class which can be readily distinguished, is
this juxtaposition of the type of name and the type of social
context anything more than a debating trick? The question
needs to be asked. Whether it can be fairly answered I am
not sure. Each reader needs to consider the evidence and
think it out for himself.

What will doubtless puzzle the novice – more particularly
when he comes to *Mythologiques* II is how on earth Lévi-
Strauss comes upon his basic oppositions in the first place.
How could it ever occur to anyone that an opposition
between roast pork and boiled cabbage might reflect a fundamental characteristic of human thinking, or that honey and
tobacco (of all things) might come to have a significance as
fundamental as that which opposes rain and drought? The
answer, I think, is that Lévi-Strauss starts at the other end.
He first asks himself: how is it and why is it that men, who
are a part of Nature, manage to see themselves as other
than Nature even though, in order to subsist, they must
constantly maintain relations with Nature? He then
observes, simply as a fact of archaeology rather than ethnography, that ever since the most remote antiquity men
have employed fire to transform their food from a natural
raw state to an artificial cooked state. Why is this? Men do
not *have* to cook their food, they do so for symbolic reasons
to show that they are men and not beasts. So fire and cooking
are basic symbols by which Culture is distinguished from

Nature. But what about the honey and tobacco? In the case of cooked food the fire serves to convert the inedible natural product into an edible cultural product; in the case of honey the fire is used only to drive away the bees, that is, to separate the food, which can be eaten raw, from its natural surroundings; in the case of tobacco it is the conversion of the food by fire into a non-substance – smoke – which makes it a food. So here already we have a set of counters of different shapes and sizes each with a front and a back which can be fitted together into patterns and which *could* be used to represent the exchanges and transformations which take place in human relations as when a *boy* becomes an *adult*, or the *sister* of A becomes the *wife* of B. With some such framework of possibilities in his mind, plus the basic proposition that mythology is concerned to make statements about the relations between Man and Nature and between man and man, Lévi-Strauss looks at his evidence and the pieces of the puzzle begin to fit together.

Because the game is unfamiliar the whole business at first seems very astonishing: there must be a catch in it somewhere. On the other hand, if Lévi-Strauss' basic assumptions were valid it could hardly be otherwise! And even if his argument eventually has to be repudiated in certain details, we simply *must* accept certain fundamental parts of it. Any knowledge that the individual has about the external world is derived from structured messages which are received through the senses ... patterned sound through the ears, patterned light through the eyes, patterned smell through the nose, and so on. But since we are aware of a *single* total experience ... *not* a sound world plus a sight world plus a smell world ... it must be because the coding of the various sensory signal systems can be made consistent – so that hearing *and* sight *and* smell *and* taste *and* touch etc. seem all to be giving the *same* message. The problem then is simply to devise a means of breaking the code. Lévi-Strauss thinks he has solved this problem; even those who have doubts can hardly fail to be astonished by the ingenuity of the exercise.

The ninth chapter of *The Savage Mind* is of a different kind from the rest and I have already made some remarks about it at pp. 22–5. Here I will do no more than repeat that what Lévi-Strauss seems to be saying is that Sartre attaches much too much importance to the distinction between history – as a record of actual events which occurred in a recorded historical sequence – and myth which simply reports that certain events occurred, as in a dream, without special emphasis on chronological sequence. History records structural transformations diachronically over the centuries; ethnography records structural transformations synchronically across the continents. In either case the scientist, as observer, is able to record the possible permutations and combinations of an interrelated system of ideas and behaviours. The intelligibility of the diachronic transformation is no greater and no less than the intelligibility of the synchronic transformations. By implication, the only way to make sense of history would be to apply to it the method of myth analysis which Lévi-Strauss is exhibiting in his study of American mythology! Whether such an argument could possibly have any appeal to professional historians or philosophers of history it is not for me to say. Certainly it lies far off the beaten track of conventional anthropology which for nearly half a century has paid little attention either to grand philosophy or to speculative interpretations of the nature of history.

So let us go back to some conventional anthropology.

6   The Elementary Structures of Kinship

And so at last we come to Lévi-Strauss' contributions to kinship theory. This is technical anthropological stuff and readers who prefer a diet of soufflé to suet pudding must mind their digestion. This part of Lévi-Strauss' work was mostly published before 1949.

I have ignored the chronology because, in this area of study, I am quite out of sympathy with Lévi-Strauss' position (see p. 18), but I must now try to explain just what the argument is all about. One long established anthropological tradition, which goes back to the publication of Morgan's *Systems of Consanguinity and Affinity of the Human Family* (1871), is to attach especial importance to the way words are used to classify genealogically related individuals. Although there are thousands of different human languages, all kin term systems belong to one or other of about half a dozen 'types'. How should we explain this? Lévi-Strauss does not follow Morgan at all closely but he assumes, as we might expect, that any particular system of kin terms is a syntagm of the 'system' of all possible systems (cf. p. 59), which is, in turn, a precipitate of a universal human psychology. This line of thought is consistent with the 'formal ethnography' of Lounsbury and others in the United States (see Scheffler, 1966: 75 f.) but is quite incompatible with the position of most British functionalist anthropologists.

If pressed, the latter will argue that the different major types of kin term system are a response to different patterns of social organization rather than to any universal attribute of the human mind.

All the same, despite their contempt for kinship words, the functionalists attach great importance to the study of kinship behaviour. There is no mystery about this. Anthropologists are usually observing human beings in situations where the facilities for transport and communication are, by modern standards, very bad. Most of the individuals under study spend their whole lives within a few miles of the locality in which they were born and in such circumstances most neighbours are biological kin. This does not mean that the people concerned will always recognize one another as kin or that they must inevitably attach special value to ties of kinship, but they may do so, and the anthropologist's experience is that this is very likely.

The general background of kinship theory lies outside the scope of this book but there is one key point which must be understood. When anthropologists talk about kinship they are concerned with *social behaviours* and not *biological facts* and the two sets of data are often so widely discrepant that it is often convenient to discuss kinship without any reference to biology. All the same, any action which is labelled 'kinship behaviour' must in the last analysis have some tenuous link with biology – it must trace back to the self-evident fact that a mother is 'related' to her own child and that brothers and sisters (siblings) of the same mother are related to one another.

Most kinship facts present themselves to the field anthropologist in two ways. In the first place as I have said his informants use a kinship terminology – words like father, mother, uncle, aunt, cousin etc. – to sort out the people in their vicinity into significant groups, but secondly it emerges that there are various sets of behaviours and attitudes which are considered especially appropriate or inappropriate as between any two individuals deemed to be related in a particular way – e.g. it may be said that a man should never speak in the presence of his mother-in-law or that it would be a good thing if he were to marry a girl who falls into the same kin term class as his mother's brother's daughter.

If we are trying to understand the day to day behaviour of people living in close face-to-face relationship, facts such as these are clearly of great significance and a good deal of the field anthropologist's research time is taken up with discovering just how these two frames of reference – the system of verbal categories and the system of behavioural attitudes – are interconnected. But for the chair-borne anthropologist, whether he be an inexperienced student or a senior professor, the data of kinship offer delights of quite another kind.

In its original context a kinship terminology is just a part of a spoken language; there is nothing very particular which separates kinship words from other words – indeed most kinship words have non-kinship meanings. Here are two examples: If you address someone as 'Father O'Brien' you probably believe that he is both celibate and childless, in the English East Anglian dialect the word 'mother' used to mean an 'unmarried girl'! However, if we ignore context, and rely exclusively on orthodox dictionary definitions the words of any kinship vocabulary can be treated as a closed set – the elements of an algebraic matrix which refers exclusively to genealogical connections. Once the words have been isolated in this way the investigator is tempted to believe that this set of terms is logically coherent, and that other sets of terms, derived in a similar way from other languages, must have a comparable coherence. In this way the analysis of kinship terminologies becomes an end in itself, to which the original facts on the ground are related only as a tiresome and perhaps misleading irrelevance.

In his earlier papers, Lévi-Strauss displayed a healthy scepticism about this sort of thing but as his own field experience recedes further into the background he has become more and more obsessed with his search for universals applicable to all humanity, and increasingly contemptuous of the ethnographic evidence. In a recent paper he has remarked, with regard to the analysis of kinship terminologies, that:

> 'F. G. Lounsbury and I. R. Buchler have proved that these nomenclatures manifest a kind of logical perfection which makes them authentic objects of scientific study; this approach has also permitted Lounsbury to expose the unreliability of some of the documentary material we are accustomed to handling without ever questioning its value' (F.K.S., 1965: 13).

My disagreement here is basic. Lévi-Strauss has said somewhere that he considers that social anthropology is a 'branch of semiology' which would imply that its central concern is with the internal logical structure of the meanings of sets of symbols. But for me the real subject matter of social anthropology always remains the actual social behaviour of human beings. Whether or not kinship nomenclatures can be regarded as 'authentic objects of scientific research' is perhaps a matter of debate, but most emphatically the logical analysis of these term systems cannot be used to determine whether any particular body of documentary material is or is not 'reliable'.

Anyway, despite these later tendencies, Lévi-Strauss' main contribution to kinship theory has not been concerned with the trivialities of kin term logic but with the structure of conventional rules of marriage. This work is of interest to all anthropologists even though its details are open to the same kind of objections as before – namely that Lévi-Strauss is liable to become so fascinated by the logical perfection of the 'systems' he is describing that he disregards the empirical facts.

The orthodox tradition of functional anthropology is to start any discussion of kinship behaviour with a reference to the elementary family. A child is related to both its parents by ties of filiation and to its brothers and sisters by ties of siblingship. These links provide the basic bricks out of which kinship systems are built up. Other discriminations depend on whether or not either parent has children by another spouse, whether or not affinal kinship (established by marriage) is or is not treated as the same as kinship based in filiation and siblingship, and so on (Radcliffe-Brown, 1952: 51).

Lévi-Strauss puts the emphasis elsewhere. Admittedly, in the vast majority of societies, a child needs to have two recognized parents before it can be accepted as a fully legitimate member of society, but the legitimacy of the child depends upon the relationship between the parents rather than the relationship between the parents and the child. So Lévi-Strauss would claim that the conventional analysis starts at the wrong place.

The average young adult (see p. 117, fig. 6) is a member of a group of siblings (A) and, as a consequence of marriage, will be brought into a new (affinal) kind of relationship with another group of siblings (B). The relationship of siblingship and the relationship of affinity are thus structurally contrasted as: + / –. As a result of the marriage, a third group of siblings (C) will be generated and this new group will be related to each of the previous groups, but *how* it will be related will depend on a variety of circumstances. All that one can say at this stage is that *If the system is one of unilineal descent, either patrilineal (C→A) or matrilineal (C→B) then the relationships between members of A and members of C must in some sense be 'the opposite of' the relationships between members of B and the members of C.*

A complete analysis of this superficially simple situation would require consideration of a wide variety of 'types' of relationship, e.g.: brother/brother, brother/sister, husband/wife, father/son, father/daughter, mother/son, mother/daughter, mother's brother/sister's son, mother's sister/sister's son, mother's brother/sister's daughter, mother's sister/sister's daughter, father's sister/brother's son, father's brother/brother's son, father's sister/brother's daughter, father's brother/brother's daughter – and already the possible permutations and combinations are enormous.

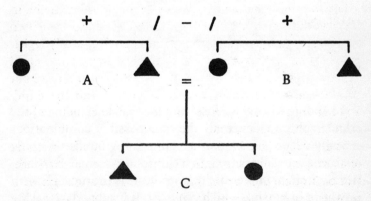

FIG. 6

But Lévi-Strauss concentrates his attention on the much more restricted set of alternatives available for two pairs of oppositions, namely the contrast between brother/sister and husband/wife on the one hand and the contrast between father/son and mother's brother/sister's son on the other. Let us represent the alternatives offered by the first opposition (X) by the words 'mutuality' (+) and 'separation' (−), and the alternatives offered by the second opposition (Y) by the words 'familiarity' (+) and 'respect' (−). Then we can draw up a matrix of possibilities of the same kind as that discussed at p. 34. Thus in Fig. 7 +/− in Column X stands for 'mutuality/separation', but +/− in Column Y stands for 'familiarity/respect'.

		X		Y	
Principle of Descent	*(Tribal Group)*	*brother/: sister*	*husband/ wife*	*father/: son*	*mB/ sisS*
MATRILINEAL	Trobriand	−	+	+	−
	Siuai,	+	−	+	−
	Dobu	+	−	+	−
PATRILINEAL	Kubutu	+	−	+	−
	Cherkess	+	−	−	+
	Tonga	−	+	−	+

FIG. 7

According to Lévi-Strauss' rather one sided reading of the ethnographic evidence all the four possible combinations actually occur (Fig. 7) and he claims, on grounds which do not seem very substantial, that this total system of possibilities is a human universal: 'this structure is the most elementary form of kinship which can exist. It is properly speaking the *unit of kinship*' and he then goes on to say that 'In order for a kinship structure to exist, three types of family relations must always be present: a relation of consanguinity, a relation of affinity and a relation of descent.'

I am bound to comment that, in my view, this argument is fallacious for a variety of reasons, the most important being that Lévi-Strauss here confuses the notion of *descent*, a legal principle governing the transmission of rights from generation to generation, with the notion of *filiation*, the kinship link between parent and child.[24] It is the same kind of confusion which led him to suppose that the incest taboo is simply the converse of exogamy (see below, p. 121).

Another point on which the argument appears vulnerable is that it is male centred, but here Lévi-Strauss finds his justification in the ethnography. He claims that his point of departure, the transaction by which a sister changes her role to that of wife, is preferable to its inverse, the transaction by which a brother changes his role to that of husband, on empirical rather than logical grounds:

> 'In human society it is the men who exchange the women, and not *vice versa*' (S.A.: 47).

To the non-anthropologist all this must seem highly artificial but for Lévi-Strauss it is a step in the direction of making the study of apparently freakish custom a problem for *scientific* investigation: or, to put it differently, it represents the establishment of a generalization from diverse particulars.

In the history of anthropology the empirical facts emerged the other way round. Lowie's early textbook (Lowie, 1920: 78) gives a long series of examples of the 'avunculate', a term which he applies somewhat indiscriminately to almost any special relationship linking a mother's brother with his sister's son. That such special relationships existed in apparently random worldwide distribution has been known to ethnographers for nearly 100 years and the most diverse explanations have been offered to account for such customs.

Some of these explanations seem to fit very well with particular sets of *local* facts (e.g. Radcliffe-Brown, 1952: Ch. 1; Goody, 1959), but the apparent merit of Lévi-Strauss' approach is that he offers a *general* theory which should apply wherever there is any ideology of unilineal descent.

Unfortunately we must at once draw a caveat. As may be seen from Fig. 7 Lévi-Strauss originally offered six positive examples to illustrate his thesis but he never considers the possibility of negative cases which do not fit his logical schema. Moreover the argument, as presented, presumes that unilineal descent systems are universal, which is wholly untrue, and, because it is untrue, Lévi-Strauss' final grandiose flourish:

> 'the avuncular relationship, in its most general form, is nothing but a corollary, now covert, now explicit, of the universality of the incest taboo' (S.A.: 51).

seems to be reduced to nonsense.

However that may be, Lévi-Strauss' major kinship treatise, *Les Structures élémentaires de la parenté* is no more than an enormously elaborated and convoluted version of this general proposition and it suffers throughout from the same defects. Logical arguments are *illustrated* by means of allegedly appropriate ethnographic evidence, but no attention whatever is paid to the negative instances which seem to abound.

The big book starts off with a very old-fashioned review of 'the incest problem' which brushes aside the substantial evidence that there have been numerous historical societies in which 'normal' incest taboos did not prevail. This allows Lévi-Strauss to follow Freud in declaring that the incest taboo is the corner-stone of human society. His own explanation of this allegedly universal natural law depends upon a theory of social Darwinism similar to that favoured by the English 19th-century anthropologist Edward Tylor. The latter maintained that, in the course of evolution, human societies had the choice of giving their womenfolk away to create political alliances or of keeping their womenfolk to themselves and getting killed off by their numerically superior enemies. In such circumstances, natural selection would operate in favour of societies enforcing rules of exogamy which Tylor equated with the converse of the incest taboo. So also does Lévi-Strauss. The error is rudimentary:

> 'the distinction between incest and exogamy ... is really only the difference between sex and marriage, and while every teenager knows the difference many anthropologists get them confused ...' (Fox, 1967: 54).

The fact is that in all human societies of which we have detailed knowledge the conventions governing sex relations are quite different from the conventions governing marriage so there is no case for saying that in the beginning the latter must have been derived from the former.

Once past this initial hurdle Lévi-Strauss goes on to discuss the logical possibilities of systems of exchange and then to consider certain rather specialized forms of marriage regulation as examples of these logical possibilities.

The argument about exchange, as such, is pretty much in line with Mauss' *Essai sur le don* (1924) and with the views of the British functionalists (e.g. Firth). The conventions of gift-giving are interpreted as symbolic expressions of something more abstract, the network of relationships which links together members of the society in question. The giving of women in marriage and the consequent forging of a special form of artificial kinship – that is to say the creation of the relationship between brothers-in-law – is seen as simply a special case, an extension in the converse direction, of the process whereby gifts of food are habitually exchanged on ceremonial occasions to express the rights and obligations of existing ties of kinship and affinity. In the jargon of Barthes' semiology (p. 58), 'gift exchange' constitutes a 'system', a general language code for the expression of relationships. 'Exchange of women' is one system within that 'system'; 'Exchange of valuables other than women' is another such system. The routine sequence of exchanges which occurs in the context of a particular marriage in a particular society is a syntagm of the 'system'. The methodology for breaking the code is the same as that which has been described in earlier chapters. The marriage systems of different societies are treated as paradigmatic transformations of an underlying common logical structure. However, Lévi-Strauss does not regard marriage (i.e. the exchange of women between men) as just one alternative system of exchange among many; it is primary. He claims that because, in the case of women, the relationship symbolized by the exchange is also constituted by the thing exchanged, the relationship and its symbol are one and the same, and the giving of women in marriage must be considered the most elementary of all forms of exchange. It must be deemed to have preceded (in evolution) the exchange of goods, where the sign and the relationship that is signified are distinct.

As with the case of the earlier avunculate argument, Lévi-Strauss' discussion of marriage rules in S.E.P. (1949) was distorted by his erroneous belief that the great majority of primitive societies have systems of unilineal descent. By now he has come to realize that this was a mistake, and there is an interesting contrast between pp. 135–6 of the first edition and pp. 123–4 of its 1967 successor. In the latter he weakly concludes:

> 'Nevertheless since this book is limited to a consideration of elementary structures, we consider it is justifiable to leave provisionally on one side examples which relate to undifferentiated filiation'(!)

Incidentally, as time goes on, it becomes increasingly difficult to understand just what Lévi-Strauss really means by 'elementary structures'. The reader needs to appreciate that the great majority of what are usually considered to be 'ultra primitive' societies (e.g. Congo Pygmies and Kalahari Bushmen) do *not* have systems of unilineal descent.[25]

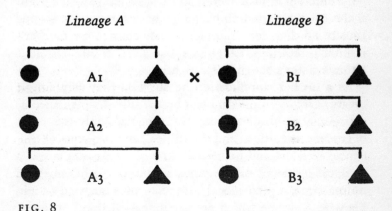

FIG. 8

However, let me try to expound Lévi-Strauss' thesis. First let us consider Fig. 8 as an elaborated form of Fig. 6 (above p. 117) in which two unilineal descent groups are represented as three generations of sibling pairs: A1, A2, A3 on the one hand and B1, B2, B3 on the other. Let us suppose that A1 and B1 are allied by marriage, either because the A1 male is married to the B1 female or vice versa, or because both of these marriages have taken place. Then, in the jargon of anthropology, the B2 siblings are classificatory first cross-cousins of the A2 siblings, while the B3 siblings are classificatory second cross-cousins[26] of the A3 siblings. Lévi-Strauss first of all considers various kinds of hypothetical marriage conventions which would have the effect of perpetuating an alliance between the A group and the B group once it had been established. If, for example, the exchange were directly reciprocal, so that the A males always exchanged sisters with the B males, then this would be the equivalent of a marriage rule expressing preference for marriage with a mother's brother's daughter or a father's sister's daughter, but a different kind of overall political structure would result if the rules required an exchange of sisters with a second cousin, so that, for example, a man marries his mother's mother's brother's daughter's daughter or his mother's father's sister's daughter's daughter.

As a further complication he suggests that very simple organizations of this kind can be usefully distinguished as 'harmonic' or 'disharmonic'. He recognizes only two types of descent: patrilineal and matrilineal, and two types of residence: virilocal and uxorilocal. In anthropological jargon a virilocal residence rule requires a wife to join her husband on marriage, an uxorilocal rule requires a husband to join his wife. Systems which are patrilineal–virilocal or matrilineal–uxorilocal are harmonic; systems which are patrilineal–uxorilocal or matrilineal–virilocal are disharmonic.

All these arguments are highly theoretical. By some stretching of the evidence some parts of the discussion can be illustrated by ethnographic facts which have been reported of the Australian Aborigines, but the latter are in no sense typical of primitive societies in other parts of the world, and there is no justification for Lévi-Strauss' apparent postulate that once upon a time all ultra primitive human societies operated in accordance with an Australian structural model. On the contrary there are good grounds for supposing that they did not.

However, for what it is worth, Lévi-Strauss maintains, on logical grounds, that harmonic structures are unstable and that disharmonic structures are stable so that systems of the first type will tend to evolve into the second type, rather than *vice versa*, or alternatively that harmonic systems of 'restricted exchange' provide the base from which have emerged harmonic systems of 'generalized exchange'. These terms need further explanation.

Lévi-Strauss classes all varieties of directly reciprocal sister exchange as falling into one major category *échange restreint* (restricted exchange) which he distinguishes from his other major category *échange généralisé* (generalized exchange). In restricted exchange, so the argument goes, a man only gives away a sister if he has a positive assurance that he will get back a wife; in generalized exchange he gives away his sister to one group but gambles that he will be able to get back a wife from some other group. The political alliance is widened – the individual gets two brothers in law where previously he had only one – but the risks are greater. Asymmetrical arrangements of this kind are equivalent to marriage rules in which marriage with one cross-cousin is approved and marriage with the other forbidden, e.g.:

1. mother's brother's daughter approved   'matrilateral cross-cousin
   father's sister's daughter forbidden   marriage rule'
   or
2. father's sister's daughter approved   'patrilateral cross-cousin
   mother's brother's daughter forbidden   marriage rule'

Rules of the second kind have just the same practical consequence as rules based on a reciprocal exchange of sisters so they are of no serious interest, though Lévi-Strauss devotes much attention to their alleged occurrence and they have been the source of much anthropological argument. Rules of the first type ('matrilateral cross-cousin marriage') are much more common, and though Lévi-Strauss was by no means the first person to bring them into serious discussion, he did manage to make a number of theoretical observations which proved to be of considerable practical significance.

FIG. 9

A matrilateral cross-cousin marriage rule, if it were strictly enforced, would produce a chain of lineages in a permanent affinal alliance of wife givers and wife receivers (Fig. 9). Such diagrams seem to contain a paradox: where will the men of Group Z get their wives? Where will the sisters of the men of Group X find their husbands?

Lévi-Strauss discusses this puzzle at enormous length. Any summary of the argument, let alone of the rival arguments produced by other authors, would be preposterously misleading but perhaps the heart of the matter is this: the system illustrated in Fig. 9, as it works out in practice, must be in some sense circular. Either the X group give their sisters to the Z group direct, or else through several intermediary groups of similar kind: in any event the women whom the Zs take in as wives are the equivalents of the women whom the Xs give away as sisters.

Lévi-Strauss recognizes that the difficulties in the way of maintaining such a system of 'circulating connubium' for any length of time must be very considerable and he claims that, in practice, the marriage circles will always break down into hierarchies such that the intermarrying lineages will be of different status. The resulting marriage system would then be hypergamous, with the groups at the top receiving women as tribute from their social inferiors.

Starting out on this fragile base, *échange généralisé* is then developed into a principle which explains the evolution of egalitarian primitive society into a hierarchical society of castes and classes.

Thus reduced, the theory sounds preposterous and even when presented at full length it is still open to all kinds of criticism of the most destructive sort, and yet there *is* an odd kind of fit between some parts of the theory and some of the facts on the ground even though, at times, the facts on the ground perversely turn Lévi-Strauss' argument back to front! For example, the systems in which hypergamous hierarchy is carried to the wildest extremes are associated with dowry rather than bride-price, while the systems in which matrilateral cross-cousin marriage is the rule mostly take the form that the wife givers rank higher than the wife receivers.[27]

Lévi-Strauss himself seems inclined to argue that if there

are *any* ethnographic facts which are consistent with his general theory, then this alone is sufficient to prove that, in its basic essentials, the general theory is right, but even his most devoted followers could hardly accept that kind of proposition.

Elsewhere Lévi-Strauss has claimed that the superiority of his method is demonstrated by the fact that a vast multiplicity of types and sub-types of human societies is here reduced to 'a few basic and meaningful principles', but he fails to point out that the vast majority of human societies are not covered by his basic and meaningful principles at all! Moreover there seems to be a major fallacy at the very root of his argument. According to Lévi-Strauss we need to think of:

> 'marriage rules and kinship systems as a sort of language that is to say a set of operations designed to ensure, between individuals and groups, a certain type of communication. The fact that the "message" would here be constituted by the *women of the group* who *circulate* between clans, lineages or families (and not, as in the case of language itself, by the *words of the group* circulating between individuals) in no way alters the fact that the phenomenon considered in the two cases is identically the same'. (A.S., 1958: 69; cf. S.A.: 61 where a different and much less literal translation is offered.)

But of course there is no such identity. If I give an object into the possession of someone else, I no longer possess it myself. Possibly I shall gain something else in exchange and possibly I retain some residual claim on the original object but I have limited my previous rights. But if I transmit a message to someone else by making a speech utterance, I do *not* deprive myself of anything at all. Having shared my information with one listener I can immediately repeat the operation and share it with another.

Certainly there is *some* kind of analogy between the two frames of reference – a collectivity of lineages which intermarry form a 'kinship community' in a sense which is, up to a point, comparable with the 'speech community' formed by any collectivity of individuals who habitually converse with one another, but, as Lévi-Strauss himself has pointed out in a different context, the concept of *mutuality* – that is of sharing common resources – is, in important respects, diametrically opposed to the concept of *reciprocity* – the exchange of distinct but equivalent resources (S.A.: 49).

However, irrespective of the merits of the particular case, the reader of this book should notice that Lévi-Strauss' over-all procedure for the analyses of marriage alliances is just the same as that which we have discussed elsewhere in the context of myth and totemism and the categories of cooking. He treats the possible preferences for marriage with a cousin of such and such a category as forming a set of logical alternatives, adherence to which will result in different over-all patterns of social solidarity within the total society. These different kinship systems, superimposed, constitute a set of paradigms (in the sense discussed at p. 60) which are manifested (a) in sets of kinship terms (b) in institutions of marriage and exchange. Taken all together the paradigms will provide us with clues as to the internalized structural logic of the human mind.

The argument is systematic: first we consider societies with two intermarrying groups, then four, then eight, then a sequence of more complex asymmetrical types. It is all so elegantly done that even the most sceptical professional may find some difficulty in detecting the precise point at which the argument runs off at a tangent. In my view the final end product is in large measure fallacious but even the study of fallacies can prove rewarding.

7 'Machines for the Suppression of Time'

Let us go back to the beginning and try to pull the argument together. Lévi-Strauss' quest is to establish facts which are universally true of 'the human mind' (*l'esprit humain*). What is *universally* true must be *natural* but this is paradoxical because he starts out with the assumption that what distinguishes the human being from the man-animal is the distinction between Culture and Nature, i.e. that the humanity of man is that which is *non-natural*. Again and again in Lévi-Strauss' writings we keep coming back to this point – the problem is not merely: 'In what way is Culture (as an attribute of humanity) *distinguishable* from Nature (as an attribute of man)?' but also 'In what way is the Culture of *Homo sapiens inseparable* from the Nature of humanity?'

Lévi-Strauss takes over from Freud the idea that it is meaningful to talk about human beings having an Unconsciousness as well as a Consciousness and, for Lévi-Strauss as for Freud, the unconscious Id is natural, the conscious Ego is cultural. When Lévi-Strauss tries to reach into 'the human mind' (*l'esprit humain*) he is grasping at the structural aspects of the Unconscious. But Lévi-Strauss' approach is through linguistics rather than through psychology. The linguistic model which Lévi-Strauss employs is now largely out of date. Present day theoreticians in the field of structural linguistics have come to recognize that the deep level process of pattern generation and pattern recognition that is entailed by the human capacity to attach complex semantic significance to speech utterances must depend on mechanisms of much greater complexity than is suggested by the digital computer model which underlies the Jakobson–Lévi-Strauss theories. Jakobson's schema of a limited set of binary distinctive features common to all human languages (see p. 38. f.) is not necessarily false but it is certainly inadequate. Where speech is concerned the ultimate objective of research is to discover not merely how children learn to distinguish noise contrasts as significant but how they acquire the generative rules which allow them to distinguish meaningful patterns of sound in the first place and what sort of rules these may be. By comparison, the patterning of manifest cultural data with which Lévi-Strauss is playing is superficial. I am ready to concede that the structures which he displays are products of an unconscious mental process but I can see no reason to believe that they are human universals. Bereft of Lévi-Strauss' resourceful special pleading they appear to be local, functionally determined, attributes of particular individuals or of particular cultural groups.[28] However, as Yvan Simonis has observed, although Lévi-Strauss originally set out to display the structure of the human mind he has ended up by telling us something about the structure of aesthetic perception.

His starting point, let us remember, was that the specifically human quality of human beings is that they have a language. At one level this allows man to communicate and form social relations and at another it is an essential element in the mysterious process we call 'thinking', in that we must first categorize our environment and then represent these categories by symbols ('elements of language' 'words') before we can 'think' about them.

This process of 'thinking' by means of word symbols (and other kinds of symbols) entails a highly complex interplay between the individual who is doing the thinking and the environment about which he is thinking. For example in our culture an essential part of almost any intellectual operation is that the thinker should be able to externalize the words and numbers which are 'in his head' and write them down on pieces of paper (or else make drawings and models of 'what he is thinking about'). Thus considered, the operation of 'thinking about' consists of the manipulation of reduced models of ideas which started out in the first place as words, which symbolize 'events' and 'things' in the environment external to the thinker. Very recently, in the last decade or so, we have carried this externalization process a step further. Having created the 'reduced model' in the form of a computer programme, we can now design machines which do a great deal of the manipulation on their own account without any immediate feed-back into the brain of the thinker at all.

In taking this step beyond ordinary verbal language and beyond ordinary written symbols, to symbols which exist 'out there' as part of the environment and which can, as it were, be made to play logical games by themselves without conscious human intervention, we seem to have almost gone full circle. Primitive man, before he had any writing, perhaps even before he had developed his spoken language to a point where it could be used as a refined instrument of logic, was already using things 'out there' as instruments with which to think. This is the essence of Lévi-Strauss' arguments about totemic species categories, and food preparation categories – they are categories which refer to things 'out there' in the human environment and they are things good for thinking not just things good to eat.

But, just as the reduced models of human thought which are 'out there' can assume many different forms – e.g. the printed page of this book conveys information in quite a different way from either a length of computer tape or the grooves of a gramophone record – so also human thought which is *internal* to the individual brain can take on different forms. When we monitor our own speech we are thinking by means of patterned sound but there are other ways also in which we treat sound patterns as 'things good for thinking'.

Completely random mixed up sound is just noise; it tells us nothing at all. But *patterned* sound of any kind will always convey information of some sort. Thus we can recognize the bark of a dog, the screech of an owl or the noise of a passing motor-bicycle. Noises of these sorts are all patterned, though the patterning is of a different kind from that of a spoken language. It is not generated by our own unconscious mental processes. But there is yet another class of patterned sounds, which we call music, which is neither speech – in any simple sense – nor noise which communicates information about the outside world. For Lévi-Strauss, music is something of a test case. Music is of human origin, not animal origin; it is part of Culture not Nature; yet it is not part of a system of exchange in the same sense that spoken language is a system of exchange; the 'meaning' of music cannot be reduced to a model or diagram in the way the 'meaning' of a kinship system or a set of myths may be reduced.

'But that music is a language by whose means messages are elaborated, that such messages can be understood by the many but sent out only by the few, and that it alone among all the languages unites the contradictory character of being at once intelligible and untranslatable – these facts make the creator of music a being like the gods and make music itself the supreme mystery of human knowledge. All other branches of knowledge stumble into it, it holds the key to their progress' (C.C.: 26; R.C.: 18).

Yet myth and music (and dreaming) have certain elements in common; they are, says Lévi-Strauss, 'machines for the suppression of time' (C.C.: 24; R.C.: 16); the last movement of a symphony is presupposed by its beginning just as the end of a myth is already implicit where it began. The repetitions and thematic variations of a musical score produce responses in the listener which depend in some way on his physiological rhythms; and, in like measure (asserts Lévi-Strauss), the repetitions and thematic variations of myth play upon physiological characters of the human brain to produce emotional as well as purely intellectual effects. Furthermore, what the individual listener understands when he hears a myth or a piece of music is in many ways personal to himself – it is the *receiver* who decides what the message is. In this respect myth and music are the converse of spoken language where it is the *sender* who decides what the message is. The structural analysis of myth and music will lead us to an understanding of the unconscious structure of the human mind because it is this unconscious (natural) aspect of the brain which is triggered into response by these special cultural (non-natural) devices:

> 'Myth and music thus appear as conductors of an orchestra of which the listeners are the silent performers' *Le mythe et l'oeuvre musicale apparaissent ainsi comme des chefs l'orchestre dont les auditeurs sont les silencieux executants* (C.C.: 25–6; R.C.: 17).

a remark which recalls Valéry's observation that poets should 'reclaim from music their rightful heritage' *reprendre à la musique leur bien* (Valéry, 1958: 42).

The massive volumes of *Mythologiques* are designed to exhibit the logical mechanisms and concealed ambiguities which evoke these emotional responses and the thesis is that when we really get down to the roots of the matter the interdependence of logical structure and emotional response is much the same everywhere – for the Nature of man is everywhere the same.

Of course there must be a sense in which Lévi-Strauss is right and yet reductionism of this degree of comprehensiveness seems to defeat its own ends. When, in the early days of psycho-analysis, the orthodox Freudians asserted as dogma the universality of the Oedipus Complex the Oedipus Complex, as such, became devoid of all analytical value. *All* evidence no matter how contradictory it might appear was forced into the pre-determined mould. And the same kind of thing seems to be happening to Lévi-Strauss. His writings display an increasing tendency to assert *as dogma* that his discoveries relate to facts which are *universal* characteristics of the unconscious process of human thought. At first this was simply a matter of generalizing from his primary schema of binary oppositions and mediating middle terms (which is little more than the Hegelian triad of thesis, antithesis, synthesis) but lately the whole system seems to have developed into a self-fulfilling prophecy which is incapable of test because, by definition, it cannot be disproved. For example, a footnote to *Mythologiques* III reports on a private communication which the author had received from the distinguished Colombian ethnographer G. Reichel Dolmatoff relating to a Choco myth which uses wild honey as a metaphor for human sperm. Since the 'philosophy of honey' which Lévi-Strauss has painfully extracted from the piled up detail of *Mythologiques* II is 'inspired by the analogy between this natural product and menstrual blood' one might have expected that Lévi-Strauss would be somewhat disconcerted, but the contrary is the case:

> 'This remarkable inversion of a system which we have revealed as occurring in a vast territory stretching from Venezuela to Paraguay does not contradict our interpretation but enriches it by a supplementary dimension . . .'
> (O.M.: 340 n.; O.T.M.: 412 n.)

But if 'supplementary dimensions' can be added to meet every contrary case then the main theory can never be put to a critical test at all.

The genuinely valuable part of Lévi-Strauss' contribution, in my view, is not the formalistic search for binary oppositions and their multiple permutations and combinations but rather the truly poetic range of associations which he brings to bear in the course of his analysis: in Lévi-Strauss' hands complexity becomes revealing instead of confusing.

It is scarcely possible to give a demonstration of revealing complexity in a book of this size but anyone who wishes to pursue my comment further should take a look at pp. 48–53 of *The Savage Mind* where Lévi-Strauss gives a digest analysis of the myths and rituals associated by the Hidatsa Indians with their techniques of catching eagles. I myself have space to quote only one paragraph. Lévi-Strauss is explaining why we can be confident that the mythical animal who first taught the Hidatsa to hunt eagles was not, as some reports have said, a bear but the wolverine (carajou). These Indians hunt eagles 'by hiding in pits. The eagles is attracted by a bait placed on top and the hunter catches it with his bare hands as it perches to take the bait. And so the technique presents a kind of paradox. Man is the trap but to play this part he has to go down into the pit, that is, to adopt the position of a trapped animal. He is both hunter and hunted at the same time. The wolverine is the only animal which knows how to deal with this contradictory situation: not only has it not the slightest fear of the traps set for it; it actually competes with the trapper by stealing his prey and sometimes even his traps. It follows . . . that the ritual importance of eagle hunting among the Hidatsa is at least partly due to the use of pits, to the assumption by the hunter of a particular *low* position (literally as we have just seen, figuratively as well) for capturing a quarry which is in the very *highest* position in an objective sense (eagles fly high) and also from a mythical point of view (the eagle being at the top of the mythical hierarchy of birds . . .)' (S.M.: 50–1).

All of which is surely very far removed from our own way of thought? But are we sure about this? Notice for example that the Hidatsa triadic schema of Sky : Earth : Underworld :: Eagles : Bait : Man–Wolverine has exactly the same 'structure' as the argument about coloured traffic lights (p. 33) with which I started this whole discussion!

Taken as a whole Lévi-Strauss' analysis shows us that, in the thinking of the Hidatsa, such practical economic matters as hunting and agriculture are inextricably entangled with attitudes towards cosmology, sanctity, food, women, life and death, and certainly this is diametrically opposed to our own contemporary fashion which lays it down that, in order to rate as rational scientists, we must keep facts and values entirely separate. Our thinking is the product of a Culture alienated from Nature: that of the Hidatsa derives from a Culture integrated with Nature.

Yet even if we concede that, with us, there can be no room for poets in the laboratory, we ought to recognize that when we set such store by objective rationality there is loss as well as gain. The poetic experience carries its own (aesthetic) rewards. Hidatsa thinking on these matters had its counterpart in the Ancient World. The underworld in which Ulysses sees and speaks with the departed heroes is no deeper than a ditch while that to which Ceres is annually abducted by Pluto has only the depth of a plough furrow; correspondingly the sky of the Ancients was no higher than the tops of some very moderate hills. When Vico commented to this effect in the early 18th century he was imbued with admiration rather than contempt; it needed the arrogance of late 19th century materialism to reduce the poetry of primitive thought to the status of a childish superstition.

But if, as Lévi-Strauss seems to be saying, Vico's 'Poetic cosmography' (Vico: 218) is a natural attribute of 'the human mind', then it should still lie somewhere within the hidden structures of our own collective unconscious. Perhaps even in the age of space rockets and hydrogen bombs Paradise need not be wholly beyond recall.

Notes

1. [JAL: In the years since Leach wrote this the total has risen to 18 books, plus another 5 (including the texts of interviews) prepared in collaboration with others. See References.]

2. Piaget *Le Structuralisme* (1968) adopts definitions which imply that Sartre is a more authentic 'structuralist' than is Lévi-Strauss! [JAL: For recent comments by Lévi-Strauss on his relationship to Marxism and to Sartre, see C.D.E.: chs 1, 4, 10, and 12. And for a more sustained, and more balanced discussion of Lévi-Strauss' place in French intellectual life in the 1950s and 1960s, see Merquior (1986).]

3. This point has been developed at length by James Boon *From Symbolism to Structuralism* (1972).

4. For further discussion see, in particular, the contributions by Ricoeur and Lévi-Strauss to the symposium debate entitled 'La Pensée sauvage et le structuralisme' in *Esprit* II, November 1963 (R). [JAL: In addition to the chapter of S.M. mentioned by Leach, interested readers will find more on Lévi-Strauss' views on history, and the historicity of what he refers to as 'so-called primitive societies' in C.G.C.: 32–42; S.A.: 1–25; S.A.:23–32; 238–55; C.D.E.: 124–5. See also note 15 below.]

5. Physicists must forgive this archaic account of the relation between colour and thermal radiation. The practical description of colour difference is highly technical but, as an example, the 'reflectances' (luminosities) of the three standard artists' colours Emerald Green, Chrome Yellow and Cadmium Red with wavelengths respectively 512, 581 and 600 millimicrons are in the ratio 2 : 3 : 1. A thermometer placed in different parts of a spectrum derived from a white light source will register the greatest temperature rise in the infra red and the least in the ultra violet.

6. In the view of many professional linguists the publication of Noam Chomsky's *Syntactic Structures* (1957) had a significance for linguistics comparable to that of Einstein's early papers on relativity theory for physics, and it has sometimes been argued, to Lévi-Strauss' dis-

credit, that in relying on a Jakobson style linguistic, he is following a model that is no longer viable. Two points need to be made on the other side. Firstly, even if Chomsky's work is an advance on that of Jakobson, it does not invalidate the genuine merits of the latter; secondly, the characteristics of Chomsky's linguistics, which are subsumed under the titles Generative and Transformational Grammars, have many points in common with the generative and transformational rules for myth analysis which Lévi-Strauss has developed on his own quite independently. But on the other side again 'the idea of a mathematical investigation of language structures, to which Lévi-Strauss occasionally alludes, becomes meaningful only when one considers rules with infinite generative capacity' (Chomsky 1968: 66). Lévi-Strauss has been concerned to demonstrate only that varieties of cultural forms, as they are actually recorded, are transformations of one another (see note 14 below). Chomsky has tackled the more fundamental problem of seeking to formulate grammatical rules which will discriminate between transformations which make acceptable sense and those which do not. Why can we say: 'the cat sat on the mat' but not 'the cat sat mat the on'?

7. For this use of the term *eidos* see Bateson (1936: 220). In Bateson's language *eidos* refers to 'a standardization of the cognitive aspects of the personality of individuals'.

8. Several critics have rebuked me for mistranslation, but in fact I cited Lévi-Strauss' own words to avoid this imputation. 'Literally' *bonnes à penser* means 'good to think', *bonnes à manger* 'good to eat'. But 'good to think' is not English, and the adjectival plural of the French is untranslatable. It seems to me that here, as so often, Lévi-Strauss is playing a verbal game. Totemic species are categories of thing, and it in fact conveys the meaning better to refer to them as 'goods' than my critics would allow. (cf. p. 134).

9. T.T. (1955): 448 'il n'a pas de place entre un *nous* et un *rien*.' [JAL: Lévi-Strauss addresses some of these issues further in V.A. (Chs. 1 and 2). Readers interested in Leach's own thoughts on these matters may consult the chapter on 'Humanity and Animality' in his book, *Social Anthropology*.]

10. The reader is expected to know that in Sartre's *Huit Clos* a character supports the opposite proposition '*l'enfer, c'est les autres*' (Garcin, during the last minute of the play).

11. It should perhaps be stressed however that, unlike Piaget, Lévi-Strauss does not speculate about the ontogenetic or philogenetic development of category systems; he simply relies on this style of argument to explain the otherwise surprising fact that he is able to discover

strikingly similar 'structures' in widely different cultural contexts.

12. It is the constant refrain of Lévi-Strauss and his close disciples that all his Anglo-Saxon critics, the present author included, are crude empiricists. 'Empiricism' here seems to mean the doctrine that truth must be verifiable by reference to observable facts; it stands opposed to 'rationalism' which reaches to a deeper form of truth by means of operations of the intellect. [JAL: It should be added a) that the ambition of reaching a 'deeper' truth beyond the reported facts, together with an impatience with others who were disinclined to do the same, are features which Leach himself displayed throughout his career; and also b) that Lévi-Strauss has frequently defended his methods on different grounds from those cited here by Leach, repeatedly insisting on the empirical and scientific nature of his inquiries. 'Only those whose entire enthnological outlook is confined to the group they have studied personally', he writes (W.M.: 145), 'are prone to overlook my almost maniacal deference to the facts'. The way Leach puts things here, as if Lévi-Strauss' interest in an algebra of possibilities must necessarily be at the *expense* of an interest in the facts of particular cases, does seem tendentious; and the implication that Lévi-Strauss explicitly declares and defends an uninterest in the 'empirical phenomena' is misleading.]

13. See note 8 above.

14. The whole of the final chapter of D'Arcy Thompson's *On Growth and Form* is highly relevant for an understanding of Lévi-Strauss' structuralism. In the 1942 edition this is Chapter XVII 'On the theory of transformations, or the comparison of related forms' (pp. 1026–1095).

15. [JAL: The contrast in position presented here by Leach between Lévi-Strauss and his 'Anglo-Saxon critics' is perhaps a bit over-drawn, and represents a false choice. (The same is true below, at p. 112, where Leach characterizes British social anthropologists as arguing that kinship terminologies 'are a response to different patterns of social organization *rather than* to any universal attribute of the human mind'). Lévi-Strauss does not deny the importance of 'adaptive evolution', 'functional relevance' or even the contingencies of history, in explaining why particular variants occur in particular contexts. He speaks (N.M.: 628) of each version of a myth as the result of a 'twofold determinism', as earlier or neighbouring versions are modified in the context of 'different techno-economic infrastructures'. (See also the discussion in S.M.: 130–1). His point is that because myths are collective phenomena, such modifications take the form over time of structural transformations, not just piece-meal or idiosyncratic emendations. Lévi-Strauss is generally much less concerned to explain how particular

transformations occurred in history than to demonstrate that the myths, marriage systems, classification, or artefacts found in different cultures are indeed transformations one of another. He claims that in most of the cases he is concerned with the data required to 'explain' each variant, in the kind of causal and historical sense Leach seems to be calling for here, are simply not available; but he is happy to make quite specific historical claims about the circumstances of his 'transformations' where he thinks the evidence is sufficient. See W.M. (especially Chapter 12) where Lévi-Strauss attempts to document how a design of mask and the origin myths associated with it, were, as he puts it, 'generated by transformation', as they passed between two peoples on the west coast of North America during the nineteenth century.]

16. This representation of the incest argument is altogether too 'empiricist'. For Lévi-Strauss the importance of the distinction exogamy/incest is that it marks the establishment of a social dichotomy order/disorder. The key myth of *Mythologiques* I, M.1, (C.C.: 43f; R.C.: 35f) and the key myth of *Mythologiques* IV, M.529/30, (H.N.: 25f; N.M.: 29f) are both manifestly 'about' incest. They are also both manifestly 'about' bird nesting. The bird nesting element entails suspension in a void between this world and the other, regression to infancy, deprivation from cooked food. Although most of the other details are quite different Lévi-Strauss declares that the two myths are *identical* but *inverse*. In M.1 a naked adolescent boy commits incest with his mother, acquires clothing, and, after adventures, kills his father; in M.529/30 the father of a richly clothed adult son strips the son of his clothing and commits incest with one of the son's many wives. In the course of adventures the son is reborn in an abnormal manner. The father is again destroyed by the son. It is only after extended analysis that these stories can be shown to be concerned with the beginning of society because they are also concerned with the beginning of time, the beginning of order, the beginning of culture. For Lévi-Strauss the most persistently recurrent 'opposition' in mythology is that between order and disorder, but it takes on endless permutations of empirical form. To illustrate this point he places near the end of *Mythologiques* I (C.C.: 318; R.C.: 312) a series of myths which move from 'noisemaking to eclipses, from eclipses to incest, from incest to unruliness, and from unruliness to the coloured plumage of birds'. The transformations which I offer in the pages which follow are of a more pedestrian kind.

17. [JAL: In general, Lévi-Strauss distinguishes between two different kinds of cross-cultural comparison. On the one hand there are compari-

sons such as those between neighbouring peoples of the North-West Coast (see note 15, above), where one can plausibly postulate historical connections between populations and so borrowing, transfer, and transformations of ideas and representations. Here he argues against the functionalist fiction of tribal 'societies' as self-contained and isolated units (e.g. N.M.: 609–10; W.M.: 144–6): arguments which Leach himself had also voiced (1954). On the other hand there are comparisons between unrelated peoples, like that between the use in the Americas, China, and Europe of musical instruments in ritual which is cited here by Leach. In an interview (C.D.E.: 129), Lévi-Strauss mentions in this connection a whimsical comparison he has made between Biblical doctrine on circumcision and what the Bororo say about their penis sheaths: 'One can't draw any conclusions, except perhaps that the human mind acts within a limited field of possibilities, so that analogous mental configurations can, without the need for invoking other causes, repeat themselves at different times and in different places. It's a bit like a kaleidoscope, which contains a finite number of translucent fragments; in theory there is nothing to prevent the reappearance of the same pattern after a certain number of turns. It is extremely unlikely, but it is not impossible.' Lévi-Strauss believes that his comparisons between myths from North and South America are nearer the former than the latter type, since the peoples of South America originally arrived there via North America. But the transformations in their mythologies happened long ago and they cannot now be demonstrated except by their effects. *The Jealous Potter* is, among other things, an extended justification of this position.]

18. In this and subsequent stories I use an anglicized Greek (rather than a Latin) spelling of personal names in the form in which they appear in the Index to Rose (1959). A summary of the leading features of the Theban myth cycle is given at pp. 86–95.

19. Compare also the following quotations:
a) 'The purpose of myth is to provide a logical model capable of overcoming a contradiction (an impossible achievement if, as it happens the contradiction is real)' (S.A.: 229).
b) 'The inability to connect two kinds of relationships is overcome (or rather replaced) by the assertion that the contradictory relationships are identical inasmuch as they are both self contradictory in a similar way' (S.A.: 216).

20. On this myth, and also on the Bororo myth from *Mythologiques I*, see note 17 above.

21. Cf. Lévi-Strauss' own formula (p. 79). In my extended analysis Incest : Fratricide-Patricide : : Murder of potential father-in-law :

Exogamy : : 'born from one' : 'born from two' : : Society in which there is no succession (Odysseus) : Society in which there is succession (Oidipus). That the Odyssey has this static implication is confirmed by consideration of a post-Homeric supplement which unsuccessfully attempts to resolve the puzzle by splitting the various roles:

Telemachos, son of Odysseus and Penelope, has a half-brother, Telegonos, son of Odysseus and Kirke. Telegonos accidentally kills Odysseus and marries Penelope; Telemachos marries Kirke.

22. [JAL: The parallel between sex and defecation, which Leach cites here from *Mythologiques II*, is developed elsewhere – especially *Mythologiques III* (O.M.; O.T.M.) – with the addition of a correspondence between cooking (itself the principal code explored in *Mythologiques I*) and digestion, another model of cultural process. And in *The Jealous Potter*, Lévi-Strauss discerns a further code in myths on the origin of pottery. This pottery code reverses that of digestion. Thus (J.P.: 175):

clay $\rightarrow$ extraction $\rightarrow$ modelling $\rightarrow$ firing $\rightarrow$ container

excrement $\leftarrow$ ejection $\leftarrow$ digestion $\leftarrow$ cooking $\leftarrow$ food

Yet like it, and the others of the *Mythologiques* series, this code deals with the passage from Nature to Culture.]

23. [JAL: This argument, that the emotions add a whole dimension to symbolic thought which Lévi-Strauss' Structuralism does not comprehend, was a prominent theme in the Anglo-Saxon response to Lévi-Strauss' work. It was developed, in addition to Leach, and of course in different ways, by Fortes (1967), Geertz (1973), Tambiah (1969), and Turner (1969). Lévi-Strauss' robust response is contained in some remarks on music and ritual at the end of the *Mythologiques* series (N.M.: 659–75). He insists that it is thought ('the work of the understanding') that elicits emotional responses, and that the idea of emotions without intellectual content is simply unexplanatory: a matter not for the social sciences but for biology.]

24. [JAL: This accusation of 'confusion' led to a heated exchange between Leach (1977) and Lévi-Strauss (1977; and S.A.2: 111–12). Perhaps the best thing to say is that the distinction between filiation and descent does not have quite the text-book simplicity and clarity claimed for it here by Leach. And the same is also true of the distinction between sex and marriage, invoked here and on p. 121. In many societies, there can be considerable ambiguity about whether two people are married or not, because a marriage is in part *made* by an ongoing conjugal relationship, instead of or as well as by a formal ceremony. In such cases any sexual relations with a person one would not be permitted to marry may be regarded as incestuous. This is the case,

indeed, reported by Leach among the Kachin, where 'illicit' hetero-sexual relations are governed, albeit somewhat less rigorously in prac-tice, by the same concepts and rules as 'marriage' (1954: 74–6; 136–8).]

25. [JAL: Actually, Lévi-Strauss is quite explicit that he does not see the presence of an elementary kinship structure as related to the 'primitiveness' or otherwise of a society: 'Let us acknowledge then that a good number of so-called primitive societies, in fact, have com-plex kinship structures' (E.S.K.: 106). So this jibe of Leach's is not really to the point. The difference, for Lévi-Strauss, between elementary structures and systems which do not have unilineal descent, is that in the former the marriage and descent rules constitute the basic struc-tural framework of the society, whereas in the latter this is provided by the system of ownership in land. It should also be noted that in the years since Leach wrote these words, Lévi-Strauss has not been content merely to acknowledge the existence of a wide range of so-called primi-tive societies, in many parts of the world, without unilineal descent; he has also devoted some effort to finding concepts to replace that of decent and descent group, in an attempt to understand their social organization. See his discussions of 'house societies' (W.M.: 163–87; A.M.: 151–94; H.E.); and see also recent uses of these ideas by anthro-pologists working in such societies (Carsten & Hugh-Jones 1995).]

26. A cross-cousin is a cousin of the type 'mother's brother's child' or 'father's sister's child' as distinct from a parallel cousin who is a cousin of the type 'mother's sister's child' or 'father's brother's child'. [JAL: i.e. where the parents of the two children include siblings of the same sex, we have parallel cousins; where the siblings are of different sexes, the cousins are cross-cousins.]

27. In the 1967 and 1969 editions of this book Lévi-Strauss attempted to mask the fact that he had ever made this ethnographic error but the resulting patchwork in his text only leads to inconsistency. See Leach (1969). [JAL: Generally, Lévi-Strauss has been sparing in his published replies to his critics, preferring to adopt a rather Olympian stance, describing 'written controversy' as 'something I continue to find equally distasteful both to read and to compose' (A.M.: 4). This self-description is belied somewhat by the texts of his replies to Leach. Consider the following: 'In 1951, E. R. Leach, a British anthropologist, adopted my interpretation, which he then undertook to defend against me while attributing to me another interpretation invented by him to further the argument' (S.A.: 320). See note 24 above. The 'patchwork' referred to here by Leach actually contains Lévi-Strauss' responses (E.S.K.: 234–45) to Leach's earlier criticisms of his use of Kachin eth-

nography, and in this Lévi-Strauss quotes Leach (1954) against Leach (1951) to some considerable effect. The arguments are detailed and, as Leach intimates here, somewhat recondite. (When he later gave an off-print of his 1969 'rejoinder to Lévi-Strauss' to one of his students, Leach marked it 'Comedy!'). The points to note are a) that wherever one thinks the errors lie in the debate, Lévi-Strauss is not really as insouciant about ethnographic accuracy as Leach implies in this book, taking trouble as he does to answer critics and insist that his theories do adequately fit the facts; and b) that while Lévi-Strauss rejects the accusation of 'blunders' by Leach, he does accept that the model of the Kachin marriage system put forward by Leach, in the works the latter wrote after reading the first edition of E.S.K., was 'infinitely preferable' to his own earlier attempt. So although both were driven some way by the imperatives of academic invective, it is clear that for both of them the other's contribution was enlightening.]

28. See note 6 above, also pp. 36–7.

References

Works by C. Lévi-Strauss:

Date	Code Reference	Title
1936	–	'Contribution à l'étude de l'organisation sociale des Indiens Bororo', *Journal de la Société des Américanistes* XXVIII fasc 2
1945	–	'L'analyse structurale en linguistique et en anthropologie', *Word* (Journal of the Linguistic Circle of New York Vol. 1 No. 2) [English version in S.A. Chapter II.]
1948	–	*La vie familiale et sociale des Indiens Nambikwara*. Paris
1949	S.E.P.	*Les Structures élémentaires de la parenté*. Paris [Revised edition 1967.]
	E.S.K.	[English version of revised edition *The Elementary Structures of Kinship*, London 1969.]
1952	–	*Race et Histoire*. Paris [English version *Race and History*, New York, 1958.]
1955	T.T.	*Tristes Tropiques*. Paris
	W.W.	[Incomplete English version *World on the Wane*, London 1961.]
	T.T.E.	[Complete English version *Tristes Tropiques*, London, 1973.]
1955	S.S.M.	'The Structural Study of Myth', *Journal of American Folklore* Vol. 68 No. 270 [Modified version in S.A. Chapter XI.]
1958	A.S.	*Anthropologie structurale*. Paris.
	S.A.	[English version *Structural Anthropology*, New York 1963, London 1968.]

1960	G.A.	'La Geste d'Asdiwal', *Annuaire de l'E.P.H.E.* (Sciences Religieuses) 1958–9, Paris [English version in S.A.2 Chapter IX.]
1960	V.P.	'La Structure et la forme. Reflexions sur un ouvrage de Vladimir Propp' *Cahiers de l'Institut des Sciences économiques appliquées.* Paris [English version in S.A.2 Chapter VIII.]
1961		edited by George Charbonnier, *Entretiens avec Claude Lévi-Strauss.* Paris
	C.G.C.	[English version *Conversations with Claude Lévi-Strauss,* London 1969.]
1962		*Le Totémisme aujourd'hui.* Paris
	T.	[English version *Totemism.* London 1964.]
1962		*La Pensée Sauvage.* Paris.
	S.M.	[English version *The Savage Mind,* 1966.]
1963	R.	'Reponses à quelques questions', *Esprit* (Paris) Novembre 1963, pp. 628–53. [English version in S.A.2. Chapter XV.]
1964	C.C.	*Mythologiques I: Le cru et le cuit.* Paris [English version of Introduction (Overture) only
	Y.F.S.	in Y.F.S. (below) pp. 41–65.]
	R.C.	[English version of full text *The Raw and the Cooked.* London 1970.]
1965	T.C.	'Le Triangle culinaire', *L'Arc* (Aix-en-Provence) No. 26, pp. 19–29 [English version in *New Society* (London) 22 December 1966, pp. 937–40.]
1965	F.K.S.	'The Future of Kinship Studies', The Huxley Memorial Lecture, *Proceedings of the Royal Anthropological Institute*
1967	M.C.	*Mythologiques II: Du miel aux cendres.* Paris
	H.A.	[English version *From Honey to Ashes*, London 1972.]
1968	O.M.	*Mythologiques III: L'origine des manières de table.* Paris
	O.T.M.	[English version *The Origin of Table Manners*, London 1978.]
1970	P.C.	Personal communications to the author
1971	H.N.	*Mythologiques IV: L'Homme nu.* Paris [English version *The Naked Man.* London 1981.]
1973		*Anthropologie structurale deux.* Paris

Lévi-Strauss

	S.A.2	[English version *Structural Anthropology 2*. New York 1976, London 1977.]
1975		*La Voie des masques*. Geneva [Enlarged edition Paris, 1979.]
	W.M.	[English version *The Way of the Masks*. Seattle 1982, London 1983.]
1977		'Réponse à Edmund Leach', *L'Homme* 17: 131–3
1983		*Le Regarde éloigné*. Paris.
	V.A.	[English version *The View from Afar*. New York 1985, Oxford 1985.]
	H.E.	'Histoire et ethnologie', *Annales* 38: 1217–31
1984		*Paroles données*. Paris
	A.M.	[English version *Anthropology and Myth*. Oxford and New York 1987.]
1985		*La Potière jalouse*. Paris.
	J.P.	[English version *The Jealous Potter*. Chicago 1988.]
1988		with Didier Eribon, *De Pres et de loin*. Paris
	C.D.E.	[English version Claude Lévi-Strauss and Didier Eribon, *Conversations with Claude Lévi-Strauss*. Chicago 1991.]
1991		*Histoire de Lynx*. Paris [English version *The Story of Lynx*. Chicago 1995.]
1993		*Regarder, écouter, lire*. Paris

Works by other authors:

Bateson, G., 1936, *Naven*, Cambridge
Barthes, R., 1967, *Elements of Semiology*, London
Boon, J. A., 1972, *From Symbolism to Structuralism*, Oxford
Carsten, J., and Hugh-Jones, S. (eds.), 1995, *About the House*, Cambridge
Chomsky, N., 1957, *Syntactic Structures*, The Hague
Chomsky, N., 1964, *Current Issues in Linguistic Theory*, The Hague
Chomsky, N., 1968, *Language and Mind*, New York
Davy, C., 1965, *Words in the Mind*, London
Ehrmann, J. (ed.), 1966, 1970 See Y.F.S. below
Empson, W., 1931, *The Seven Types of Ambiguity*, Cambridge
Fortes, M., 1967, 'Totem and Taboo', *Proceedings of the Royal Anthropological Institute for 1966*
Fox, R., 1967, *Kinship and Marriage*, London
Frazer, J. G., 1922, *The Golden Bough* (Abridged Edition), London
Geertz, C., 1973, 'The Cerebral Savage', in *The Interpretation of Cultures*, New York

Goldenweiser, A., 1910, 'Totemism, an Analytical Study', *Journal of American Folklore*, Vol. 23

Goody, J., 1959, 'The Mother's Brother and the Sister's Son in West Africa', *J. R. Anthrop. Inst.* 89: 61–88

Hultkrantz, A., 1957, *The North American Indian Orpheus Tradition*, Stockholm

Jakobson, R., & Halle, M., 1956, *Fundamentals of Language*, The Hague

Lane, M. (ed.), 1970, *Structuralism: a Reader*, London

Leach, E., 1951, 'The Structural Implications of Matrilateral Cross-Cousin Marriage', *Journal of the Royal Anthropological Institute* 81: 54–104

Leach, E., 1954, *Political Systems of Highland Burma*, London

Leach, E., 1961, *Rethinking Anthropology*, London.

Leach, E., 1964, 'Anthropological Aspects of Language: Animal Categories and Verbal Abuse', in (E. H. Lenneberg ed.) *New Directions in the Study of Language*, Cambridge Mass.: 23–63

Leach, E., 1967, 'Brain Twister', *New York Review of Books*, 9/6, October 12, 1967: 6–10

Leach, E., 1969, 'Kachin and Haka Chin: a Rejoinder to Lévi-Strauss', *Man* (N.S.) 4: 277–85

Leach, E., 1977, 'The Atom of Kinship, Filiation, and Descent: Error in Translation or Confusion of Ideas?', *L'Homme*, 17: 127–9

Leach, E., 1982, *Social Anthropology*, London

Lowie, R., 1920, *Primitive Society*, New York

Maranda, P., and E. K. (eds.), 1971, *Structural Analysis of Oral Tradition*, Philadelphia

Marc-Lipiansky, M., 1973, *Le Structuralisme de Lévi-Strauss*, Paris

Mauss, M., 1924, 'Essai sur le don', *L'Année sociologique, Seconde serie*, 1923–24 [English version *The Gift* (1954), London.]

Merquior, J. G., 1986, *From Prague to Paris: A Critique of Structuralist and Post-Structuralist Thought*, London

Morgan, L. P., 1871, *Systems of Consanguinity and Affinity of the Human Family*, Washington

Paz, O., 1970, *Claude Lévi-Strauss: an Introduction*, London

Piaget, J., 1971, *Structuralism*, London

Pouillon, J., 1965, 'Sartre et Lévi-Strauss', *L'Arc No. 26* Aix-en-Provence, pp. 55–60

Pouillon, J., and Maranda, P. (eds.), 1970, *Echanges et Communications* 2 Vols. The Hague

Radcliffe-Brown, A. R., 1929, 'The Sociological Theory of Totemism', reprinted as Chapter VI of Radcliffe-Brown (1952)

Radcliffe-Brown, A. R., 1951, 'The Comparative Method in Social Anthropology', *J. R. Anthrop. Inst.* 81: 15–22

Radcliffe-Brown, A.R., 1952, *Structure and Function in Primitive Society*, London

Ricoeur, P., 1963, 'Structure et herméneutique', *Esprit* (Paris), Novembre 1963, pp. 596–627

Robey, D. (ed.), 1973, *Structuralism: an Introduction*. Oxford

Rousseau, J. J., 1783, 'Essai sur l'origine des langues', Geneva

Sartre, J.-P., 1960, *Critique de la raison dialectique*, Paris

Saussure, F. de, 1959, *Course in General Linguistics*, New York

Scheffler, H., 1966, 'Structuralism in Anthropology' in Y.F.S. (below), pp. 66–88

Schniewind, J., 1953, 'A Reply to Bultmann' in H. W. Bartsch (Editor), *Kerygma and Myth*, London

Simonis, Y., 1968, *Claude Lévi-Strauss ou la passion de l'inceste: Introduction au structuralisme*, Paris

Steiner, G., 1967, *Language and Silence*. London

Tambiah, S. J., 1969, 'Animals are Good to Eat and Good to Prohibit', *Ethnology*, 8: 423–59

Thompson, D. A. N., 1942, *On Growth and Form*, Cambridge

Turner, V. W., 1969, *The Ritual Process*, Chicago

Valéry, P., 1958, *Paul Valéry: the Art of Poetry (The Collected Works of Paul Valéry*, Vol. VII edited J. Mathews), New York, London

Van Gennep, A., 1920, *L'Etat actuel du problème totémique*, Paris

Vico, G., 1744 (1961), *The New Science of Giambattista Vico* [Anchor Books edn. New York.]

White, L., 1949, *The Science of Culture*, New York

Y.F.S., 1966, *Structuralism* (Edited Jacques Ehrmann) [Double issue of *Yale French Studies*, Nos. 36, 37, New Haven; also published by Anchor Books, New York, 1970.]

Guide to Further Reading
by James Laidlaw

Commentaries by anthropologists on the work of Lévi-Strauss are now very numerous. The following will give a representative range of opinions. James Boon, 'Claude Lévi-Strauss' in (Quentin Skinner ed.), *The Return of Grand Theory* (Cambridge 1985); Clifford Geertz, 'The Cerebral Savage', in *The Interpretation of Cultures* (New York 1973); Clifford Geertz, 'The World in a Text', in *Works and Lives* (Oxford 1988); Ernest Gellner, 'What is Structuralism?' in *Relativism and the Social Sciences* (Cambridge 1985); Dan Sperber, 'Absent Meaning', in *Rethinking Symbolism* (Cambridge 1975); Dan Sperber, 'Claude Lévi-Strauss Today', in *On Anthropological Knowledge* (Cambridge 1985). Significant in a different way, and among the founding texts of 'post-structuralism', are Jacques Derrida's discussions of Lévi-Strauss. See 'Structure, Sign and Play in the Discourse of the Human Sciences' in *Writing and Difference* (Chicago 1978) and *Of Grammatology* (Baltimore 1976).

The real question is which of Lévi-Strauss' own works should the interested reader tackle? And the answer depends on what his or her interest is.

Tristes Tropiques was published in 1955 when, as Lévi-Strauss has subsequently claimed, he thought he did not have an academic career before him. It is a book of memoirs and reflections and is an enchanting introduction to a singular sensibility. The second English translation (1973) is the one to read.

Those interested in Lévi-Strauss' method of analysis will find in *Totemism* (1964; French original, 1962) a clear, indeed a rather didactic and programmatic exposition, and an illustration of how Lévi-Strauss' approach differed from that of his predecessors. Other general statements by Lévi-Strauss of his principles and methods can be found in 'Structural Analysis in Linguistics and Anthropology' and 'Social Structure' (both in *Structural Anthropology*); and in 'The Scope of Anthropology' (in *Structural Anthropology 2*).

An aspect of Lévi-Strauss' writing which is not really touched upon by Leach is his approach to the visual arts. He has written quite extensively on so-called 'primitive art' as well as on European Classicism and Modernism. There are essays in *Structural Anthropology* and *The View from Afar;* his monograph on the indigenous art of the North-West Coast, *The Way of the Masks;* extensive comments in the two volumes of 'conversations' listed in the references; and much, including an essay on Poussin, in *Regarder, écouter, lire.*

To enter the world of Lévi-Straussian myth analysis the logical route to take would be to follow the chronology of Lévi-Strauss' writing, beginning with 'The Structural Study of Myth' (in *Structural Anthropology*), then 'The Story of Asdiwal' (in *Structural Anthropology 2*), *The Savage Mind*, and then on to *The Raw and the Cooked*, the first of the *Mythologiques* series. But I would recommend, instead, that readers who feel they have followed Leach proceed straight to *The Jealous Potter* (1988; French original 1985). Unlike the *Mythologiques*, this is a book which even ordinary mortals can imagine finishing; yet it lacks nothing of their range – geographical, imaginative, and thematic. Where some of the earlier works are dry and programmatic, this book is clever, ingenious, and witty. In *The Jealous Potter* Lévi-Strauss also returns, in an unexpected way, to the Oedipus myth – the example used in 'The Structural Study' and developed by Leach in this book. And by this route he comes to a brief discussion of Freud, so that the thinker who is cited in *Tristes Tropiques* as one of the formative influences on Lévi-Strauss' thinking is finally put, structurally, in his place.

Index

Lévi-Strauss